PLASTIC CANVAS

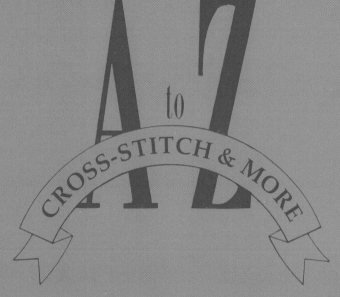

A to Z

CROSS-STITCH & MORE

Vanessa-Ann's
PLASTIC A to Z CANVAS
CROSS-STITCH & MORE

Meredith® Press
New York, New York

Dear Crafter:

Meredith Press is delighted to bring you *Plastic Canvas A to Z* from the multi-talented designers at The Vanessa-Ann Collection.

Within these pages you'll find a spectacular collection of exciting three-dimensional projects that combines the form and function available with plastic canvas, with beautiful needlepoint designs and creative new ideas.

We at Meredith Press are dedicated to bringing you the highest quality craft books filled with wonderful projects, exquisite color photographs and clear, easy-to-follow charts and instructions.

We wish you many happy hours stitching your way through the alphabet with *Plastic Canvas A to Z* and the enjoyment of the treasured keepsakes you create.

Sincerely,

Pat Van Note

Pat Van Note
Product Development Manager

ISBN: 0-696-02347-4
First Printing: 1991
Library of Congress Catalog number: 89-063578

Published by Meredith® Press

Distributed by Meredith Corporation, Des Moines, Iowa

1 0 9 8 7 6 5 4 3 2 1

All rights reserved

Printed in the United States of America

Pat,
We would like to dedicate this book to you because you were the one who saw something in us that even we couldn't see!
We love you,
Jo and Tece

For Meredith® Press
Director: Elizabeth P. Rice
Product Development Manager: Patricia Van Note
Editorial Project Manager: Barbara S. Machtiger
Production Manager: Bill Rose

For The Vanessa-Ann Collection
Owners: Jo Packham and Terrece Beesley

Designers: Terrece Beesley, Trice Boerens, Joan Green, Cheryl Montgomery Hofe, Jo Packham, Carole Rodgers, Florence Stacey

Staff: Ana Ayala, Tricia Barney, Gloria Baur, Vicki Burke, Sandra D. Chapman, Tim Fairholm, Holly Fuller, Susan Jorgensen, Margaret Shields Marti, Barbara Milburn, Lisa Miles, Caryol Patterson, Reva Smith Petersen, Pam Randall, Florence Stacey, Gayle Voss, Nancy Whitley

Photographer: Ryne Hazen

The Vanessa-Ann Collection thanks Mary Gaskill at Trends and Traditions in Ogden, Utah; Brigham Street Inn in Salt Lake City, Utah; and Diana and Ralph Dunkley of Ogden, Utah, for allowing us to photograph in their businesses and home.

Contents

When you were young, it was plain to see,
One of the first things you learned was your ABCs.
But now you're wiser, and although plastic canvas is new,
It's still your ABCs that will see you through.

 A is for an angel dressed in shiny, all white "lace";
She can adorn a Christmas tree or other special place.
And one thing that is certain, it's true and you will see,
This tiny tree top angel will your favorite always be.

Angel on High

Finished size: 8" W x 10½" H

Materials

Materials for stitching (see Codes)
Scrap of white satin
1 card of Sew Your Wild Threads Emotion
    thread #218
1 (1½"-diameter) wood bead
Acrylic paints: white, green, red
Glue gun and glue

Directions

1. Stitch and trim plastic canvas pieces as directed in Codes.

2. Using stitched Sleeve as a pattern, cut two pieces from satin, adding ¼" seam allowances to all edges (Sleeve lining).

3. Overcast short edges of Skirt together. For Sleeves, match As (see graph) and overcast together. Repeat for Bs. Overcast short edges of Bodice. Overcast two Wings together with wrong sides facing and edges aligned.

4. With wrong sides facing, match As and Bs of Sleeve lining and stitch. Press remaining edges under ¼". Turn. Insert one lining in each plastic canvas Sleeve, matching outside edges. Whipstitch outside edges.

5. Whipstitch Sleeves to Bodice. Tack top edges of Bodice together to form shoulders. Center and whipstitch Wings to back of Bodice. Tack top edges of Skirt together to form waist. Whipstitch Bodice to Skirt at waist.

6. Paint bead white; allow to dry. Paint face as follows: eyes, green; nose, light green; mouth, red (see Face Pattern). Center and

glue bead to top of Bodice. For hair, make 2" loops using Emotion thread. Then glue to bead until completely covered.

Codes

Stitch on clear Plastic Canvas 7 over one bar.

	Cut Size
Wing (cut and stitch two)	9" x 7"
Sleeve (cut and stitch two)	6" x 6"
Bodice (cut and stitch one)	8" x 5"
Skirt (cut and stitch one)	15" x 9"

STEP 1: Cross-stitch (one strand)

Spools		Balger #32 (heavy) Braid
1	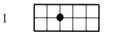	Pearl

STEP 2: Double cross-stitch (one strand)

		Balger ⅟₁₆" Ribbon
2		032 Pearl

STEP 3: Trim and overcast (one strand)

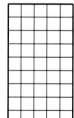

Balger #32 (heavy) Braid

    Pearl (Skirt, Sleeves and
    Bodice, see Step 3
    of Directions)

Balger ⅟₁₆ " Ribbon

032   Pearl (Wings, see Step
      3 of Directions)

Face Pattern

STEP 4: Couching—Cut white fabric into ½" x 36" strips. Using one fabric strips and one strand of Estaz of equal length, make ¾" loops and couch between every three bars with pearl cotton.

Yards		Fabric	
¾			White
Cards		**Estaz**	
16		01	Pearl
Skeins		**DMC Pearl Cotton #5**	
1			White

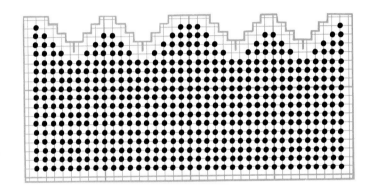

Bodice
Stitch Count: 39 x 19

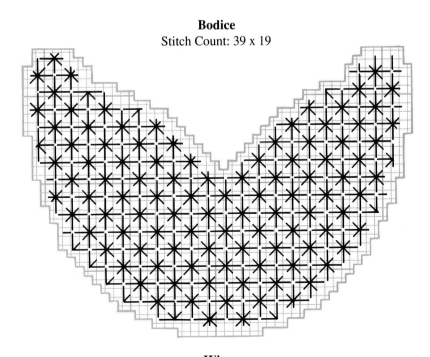

Wing
Stitch Count: 46 x 33

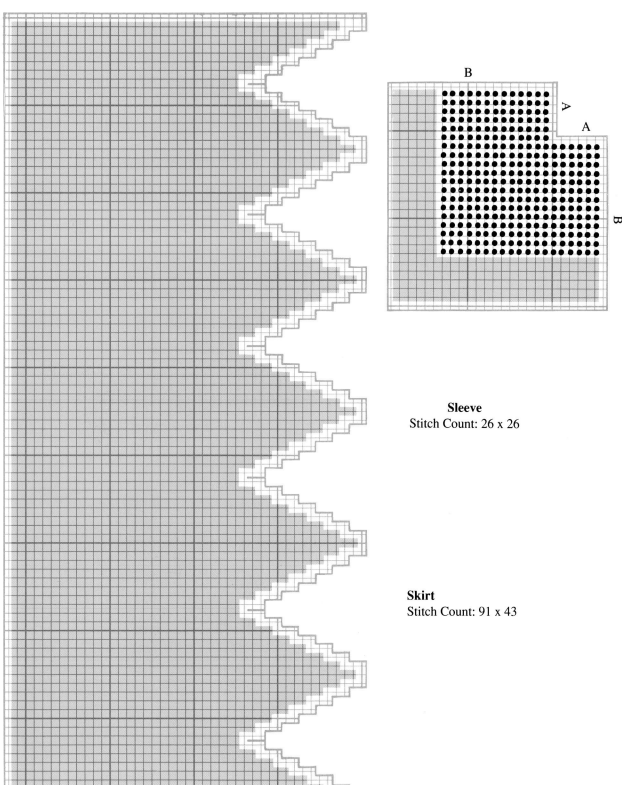

Sleeve
Stitch Count: 26 x 26

Skirt
Stitch Count: 91 x 43

B is for the butterflies which land upon your plate,
Making any mealtime fare more than just look great.
There are a set of cubes, or blocks if you do like,
That are made for all the children from Sally up to Mike

ABC Blocks

Finished size: Blocks A, B and C—4" x 4"

BLOCK A

Stitch on clear Plastic Canvas 7 over one bar. The plastic canvas is cut 4½" x 4½" for each side. Cut and stitch Sides 1 through 6.

STEP 1: Cross-stitch (two strands)

Skeins		Sides 1, 2, and 3 Paternayan Persian Yarn	
1	—	260	White
1	●	764	Daffodil-vy. lt.
1	⨯	560	Glacier-vy. dk.
1	✕	592	Caribbean Blue-med.
2	▪	591	Caribbean Blue-dk.
1	⊖	533	Blue Spruce
2	▢	464	Beige Brown-lt.
2	■	463	Beige Brown
1	✖	246	Neutral Gray

Cards		Overture (three strands)	
1	—	V55	Monarch

Cards		Sew Your Wild Threads (two strands)	
1	⊙	609	Passion

Paternayan Persian Yarn
Side 4 Checkerboard

2	⊕	475	Toast Brown-vy. lt.
	■	463	Beige Brown

Side 5 Checkerboard

4	⊕	444	Golden Brown-lt.
	■	463	Beige Brown

Side 6 Checkerboard

Skeins			
	⊕	444	Golden Brown-lt.
1	■	344	Periwinkle-vy. lt.

STEP 2: Turkish tufting stitch (three strands)

Skeins		Paternayan Persian Yarn	
1		532	Blue Spruce-med.

STEP 3: Couched long stitch (one strand)

Cards		Sew Your Wild Threads	
1		909	Strip

STEP 4: Buttons

¾"-diameter buttons		Buttons
1	▲	Cream (upper left corner of box around "A")
2	▲	Lt. Brown (on each side of cream button)
4	▲	Dk. Brown (all else)

STEP 5: Trim and overcast (three strands, all edges)

Skeins		Paternayan Persian Yarn	
1		343	Periwinkle (Sides 4 and 6)
1		575	Turquoise-dk. (Sides 2 and 3)
		464	Beige Brown-lt. (Sides 1 and 5)

STEP 6: Whipstitch (three strands). To construct block, whipstitch all sides together to make a cube, leaving top open. Stuff moderately. Whipstitch opening closed.

		575	Turquoise-dk.
		464	Beige Brown-lt.

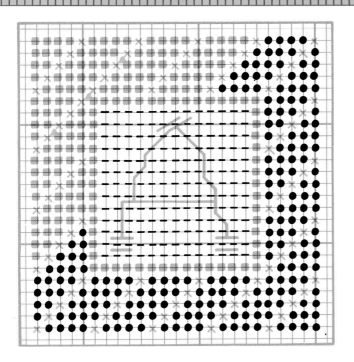

Block A, Side 1
Stitch Count: 27 x 27

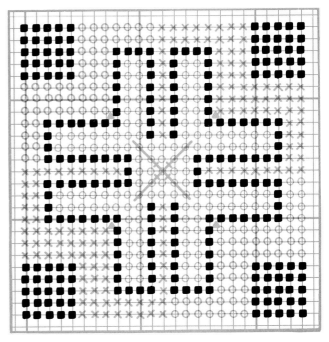

Block A, Side 2
Stitch Count: 27 x 27

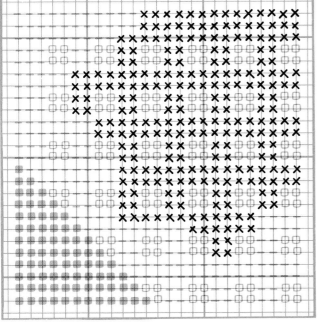

Block A, Side 3
Stitch Count: 27 x 27

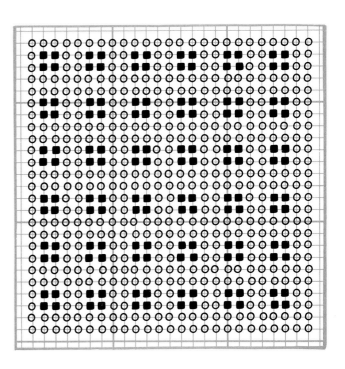

Blocks A, B, and C, Sides 4, 5, and 6
(Checkerboard)
Stitch Count: 27 x 27

BLOCK B

Stitch on clear Plastic Canvas 7 over one bar. The plastic canvas is cut 4½" x 4½" for each side. Cut and stitch Sides 1 through 6.

STEP 1: Cross-stitch (three strands)

Skeins		*Sides 1, 2, and 3* **Paternayan Persian Yarn**	
4	⊕	263	Cream
1	✹	764	Daffodil-vy. lt.
2	■	486	Terra Cotta-vy. lt.
1		840	Salmon-vy. dk.
3		564	Glacier-vy. lt.
2		562	Glacier-med.
1		561	Glacier-dk.
1		594	Caribbean Blue-lt.
1		593	Caribbean Blue
1		533	Blue Spruce
1	●	237	Silver Gray

Skeins		**Windrush Yarn**	
1		90592	Jade-med.

Paternayan Persian Yarn
Side 4 (Checkerboard, pg. 17)

3	⊕	474	Toast Brown-lt.
1	■	555	Ice Blue-lt.

Side 5 (Checkerboard, pg. 17)

	⊕	263	Cream
	■	564	Glacier-vy. lt.

Side 6 (Checkerboard, pg. 17)

	⊕	263	Cream
	■	486	Terra Cotta-vy. lt

STEP 2: Continental stitch (one strand)

Skeins		**Acadia Yarn**	
1	╱	2116	Off White

STEP 3: Backstitch (one strand)

Skeins		**DMC Matte Cotton**	
1		2407	Pecan

STEP 4: Long stitch (one strand)

	✕	2407	Pecan
	▎	2407	Pecan

STEP 5: Couched long stitch (three strands)

Skeins		**Paternayan Persian Yarn**	
		533	Blue Spruce
1		592	Caribbean Blue-med. couched with
1		570	Navy Blue-vy. lt. (one strand)

STEP 6: Woven stitch (three strands)

		593	Caribbean Blue
		592	Caribbean Blue-med.

STEP 7: Ribbon

Yards		**¹⁄₁₆ "-wide Satin Ribbon**	
2		346	Jade

STEP 8: Turkish tufting stitch (three strands)

		Paternayan Persian Yarn	
		764	Daffodil-vy. lt.
	△	564	Glacier-vy. lt.

STEP 9: Trim and overcast (three strands; all edges)

		486	Terra Cotta-vy. lt.
		562	Glacier-med.
		594	Carribean Blue-lt.

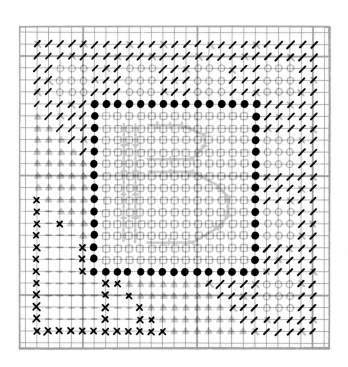

STEP 10: Whipstitch (three strands). To construct block, whipstitch all sides together to make a cube, leaving top open. Stuff moderately. Whipstitch opening closed.

Paternayan Persian Yarn

474   Toast Brown-lt.

Block B, Sides 4, 5 and 6 on page 13

Block B, Side 1
Stitch Count: 27 x 27

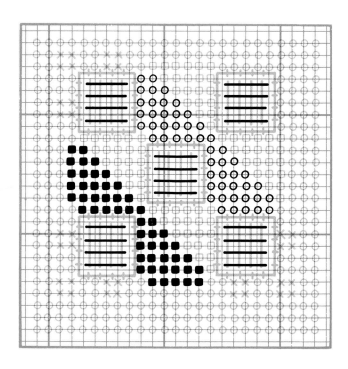

Block B, Side 2
Stitch Count: 27 x 27

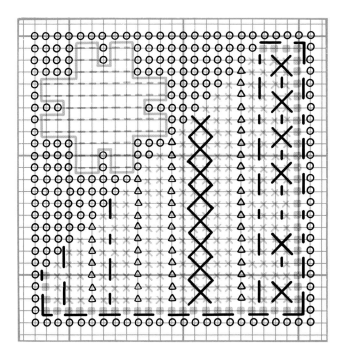

Block B, Side 3
Stitch Count: 27 x 27

BLOCK C

Stitch on clear Plastic Canvas 7 over one bar. The plastic canvas is cut 4½" x 4½" for each side. Cut and stitch Sides 1 through 6.

STEP 1: Cross-stitch (three strands)

Skeins		Sides 1, 2, and 3 Paternayan Persian Yarn	
1	—	263	Cream
2	●	490	Flesh-vy. dk.
3	■	486	Terra Cotta-vy. lt.
1		343	Periwinkle
1		562	Glacier-med.
2	□	575	Turquoise-dk.
1	×	532	Blue Spruce-med.
2	⊡	464	Beige Brown-lt.

Balls		Cotonella (one strand)	
1		C6195	Turquoise

Paternayan Persian Yarn
Side 4 (Checkerboard, pg. 17)

2	⊕	525	Teal Blue-vy. lt.
2	■	555	Ice Blue-lt.

Side 5 (Checkerboard, pg. 17)

2	⊕	494	Flesh-vy. lt.
	■	555	Ice Blue-lt.

Side 6 (Checkerboard, pg. 17)

2	⊕	764	Daffodil-vy. lt.
	■	486	Terra Cotta-vy. lt.

STEP 2: Backstitch (one strand)

Skeins		DMC Pearl Cotton #5	
1		355	Terra Cotta-dk.

Paternayan Persian Yarn

	532	Blue Spruce-med.

STEP 3: Long stitch (one strand)

DMC Pearl Cotton #5

	355	Terra Cotta-dk.

STEP 4: Couched long stitch (three strands)

Paternayan Persian Yarn

	532	Blue Spruce-med.

STEP 5: Double cross-stitch (one strand)

Skeins		DMC Matte Cotton	
1		2758	Terra Cotta-lt.

STEP 6: Buttons

½ "- diameter buttons		Buttons	
4			Peach

STEP 7: Bows. Cut bias strips into 1½" pieces. Thread through stitching and tie a knot to form bow.

⅛ "-wide bias strips			
10			Lavender

STEP 8: Trim and overcast (three strands, all edges)

	Paternayan Persian Yarn	
	490	Flesh-vy. dk.
	343	Periwinkle
	562	Glacier-med.
	464	Beige Brown-lt.

STEP 9: Whipstitch (three strands). To construct block, whipstitch all sides together to make a cube, leaving top open. Stuff moderately. Whipstitch opening closed.

	464	Beige Brown-lt.

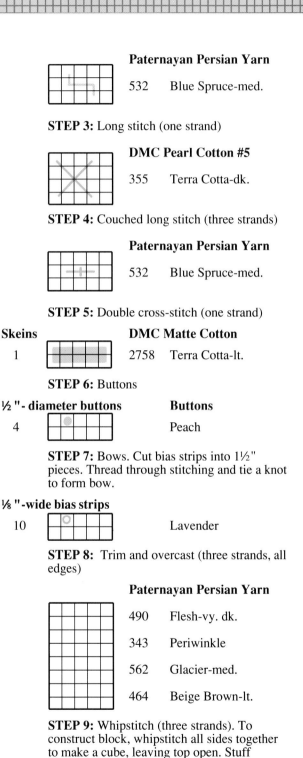

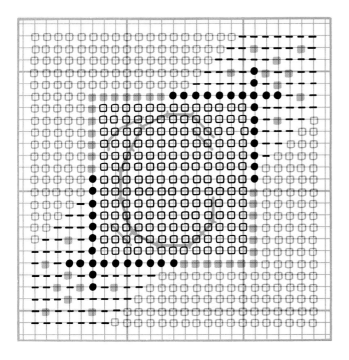

Block C, Side 1
Stitch Count: 27 x 27

Block C, Side 2
Stitch Count: 27 x 27

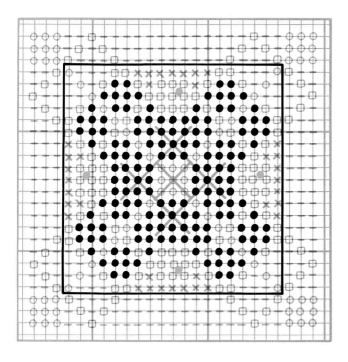

Block C, Side 3
Stitch Count: 27 x 27

Block C, Sides 4, 5 and 6 on page 13

Bountiful Butterflies

Finished size: 3" W x 3" H

Directions

1. Stitch and trim plastic canvas pieces as directed in Codes.

2. Using DMC floss #561, whipstitch Leaf/ Ring together (Diagram 1).

Diagram 1

3. Using DMC floss #340, whipstitch Wings A to A together, matching straight edges. Repeat for Bs and Cs. Cut one 4" piece each of braid and cording. Twist braid and cording together. Tie a large knot at one end for head. Fold ½" under on opposite end. Center and glue body between butterfly wings on whipstitched seam. Glue stamen, forming a V for antennae (see photo).

4. Tack butterfly to napkin ring. Placement of butterfly is indicated by the ● on the Leaf/ Ring graph.

Codes

Stitch on clear Plastic Canvas 10 over one bar.

	Cut Size
Wings	
A (cut and stitch two)	4" x 6"
B (cut and stitch two)	4" x 5"
C (cut and stitch two)	4" x 5"
Leaf/Ring (cut and stitch three)	4" x 8"

STEP 1: Cross-stitch (four strands)

Skeins		DMC Floss	
1	⬥	3078	Golden Yellow-vy. lt.
1	—	754	Peach-lt.
1	⊕	353	Peach
1	✖	3689	Mauve-lt.
1	■	3354	Dusty Rose-vy. lt.
1	┤	211	Lavender-lt.
3	▣	340	Blue Violet-med.
1	⊙	598	Turquoise-lt.
1	✳	597	Turquoise
1	⊙	913	Nile Green-med.
1	✕	562	Jade-med.
2	▦	561	Jade-vy. dk.

STEP 2: Backstitch (one strand)

	340 Blue Violet-med. (wings)

STEP 3: Trim and overcast (four strands)

	340 Blue Violet-med. (Wings)
	561 Jade-vy. dk. (Leaf/Ring)

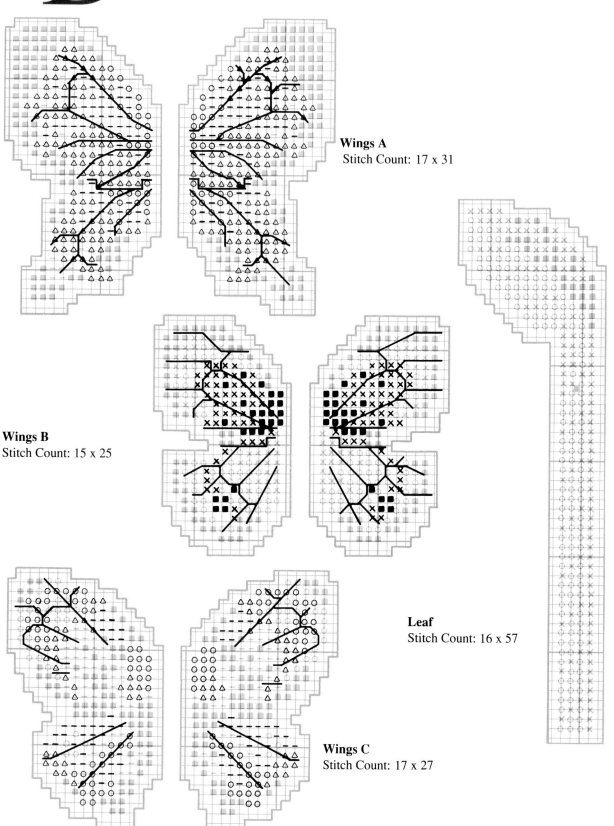

Wings A
Stitch Count: 17 x 31

Wings B
Stitch Count: 15 x 25

Leaf
Stitch Count: 16 x 57

Wings C
Stitch Count: 17 x 27

C is for carousel and music it does play,
Like a pretty song bird in the merry month of May.
The bunny and the cart are for someone oh, so fine!
To say that I do love you, and won't you please be mine?

Country Cart

Finished size: 11½" W x 4" H x 4" D

Materials

Materials for stitching (see Codes)
Overture thread
4 (2½"-wide) wood bunnies*
Stuffed fabric vegetables*:
    10 tomatoes
    2 rutabagas
    4 carrots
    5 cabbages
1 package of Spanish moss*
Glue gun and glue
*available at craft stores

Directions

1. Stitch and trim plastic canvas pieces as directed in Codes.

2. To make cart, overcast short edges of Ends and Sides together to form an open box. Overcast Bottom to straight edge of box to make cart.

   Align edges and overcast two Wheels together. Repeat. Glue one wheel to each side, with center spoke parallel to bottom edge of cart.

   Align edges and overcast one Handle A to one Handle B with wrong sides facing. Repeat. Glue one handle to each side of cart 1¼" from front edge and 1⅝" from bottom.

3. Align and overcast Stand pieces with wrong sides facing. Place wide end of stand 1¼" above bottom edge of cart and centered horizontally; glue.

4. Braid three 10" pieces of thread together, leaving 3" tails at each end. Thread tails through center of each curved end of handle knotting tails on outside edge to secure (see photo).

5. Stuff cart with moss to within 1" of top edge of cart. Place bunnies and vegetables in cart as desired (see photo).

Codes

Stitch on brown Plastic Canvas 10 over one bar.

	Cut Size
Stand (cut and stitch two)	4" x 5"
Wheel (cut and stitch four)	6" x 6"
Handle A (cut and stitch two)	10" x 3"
Handle B (cut and stitch two)	10" x 3"
Bottom (cut and stitch one)	7" x 6"
End (cut and stitch two)	6" x 5"
Side (cut and stitch two)	8" x 5"

STEP 1: Continental stitch (two strands)

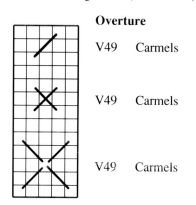

Cards		Overture	
5		V49	Carmels
Skeins		**DMC Pearl Cotton #3** (two strands)	
2		840	Beige Brown-med.

STEP 2: Long stitch (two strands)

	Overture	
	V49	Carmels
	V49	Carmels
	V49	Carmels

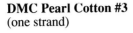

DMC Pearl Cotton #3
(one strand)

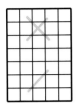

840   Beige Brown-med.
(Wheels)

840   Beige Brown-med.

STEP 3: Upright cross (two strands)

Overture

V49   Carmels

STEP 4: Cross-stitch (two strands)

V49   Carmels

STEP 5: Cross-stitch Bottom (two strands).
Stitch 45 x 29 stitches (there is no graph for
this piece).

V49   Carmels

STEP 6: Trim and overcast (two strands)

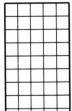

V49   Carmels (Ends, Sides,
Bottom and Handles,
see Step 2 of Directions)

DMC Pearl Cotton #3
(two strands)

840   Beige Brown-med.
(Wheels, see Step 2 of
Directions; Stand, see
Step 3 of Directions)

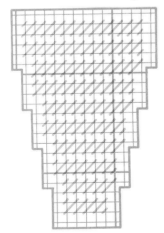

Stand, Stitch Count: 15 x 22

Handle A
Stitch Count: 76 x 9

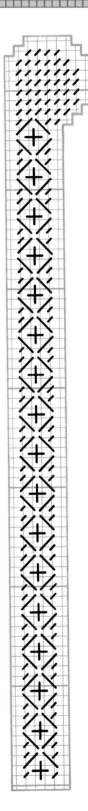

Handle B
Stitch Count: 76 x 9

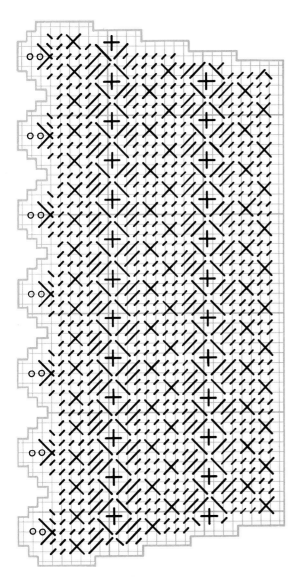

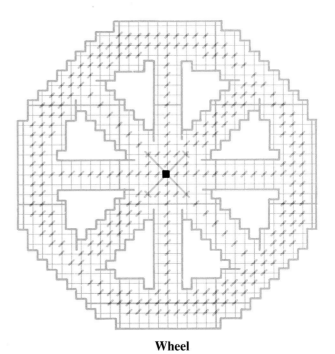

Wheel
Stitch Count: 31 x 31

Side
Stitch Count: 55 x 28

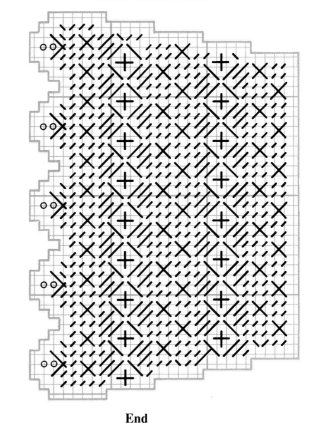

End
Stitch Count: 39 x 28

Carousel Fantasy

Finished size: 5½" W x 10½" H x 5½" D

Materials

Materials for stitching (see Codes)
5¼ yards of ⅛"-wide mauve silk ribbon*
¾ yard each of ⅛"-wide light green and blue
    silk ribbon*
3 (3½" x 3½") unpainted ceramic carousel
    horses (available at craft stores)
1 (1½"-diameter) wood bead with a hole
    through the center
1 (17¼" x 1¼) piece of corrugated cardboard
1 (9½" x ⅝") piece of corrugated cardboard
Music box movement #572
Stuffing
Assorted pastel acrylic paints
Glue gun and glue
*see Suppliers

Directions

1. Stitch and trim plastic canvas pieces as directed in Codes.

2. Paint ceramic horses as desired (see photo). Set aside.

3. Stuff Pole to within ½" of each end. Overcast inner edge of Circle A to one end of Pole. Overcast inner edge of Circle B to opposite end of Pole.

4. Overcast short edges of Base Band together to make a circle. Glue music box movement to wrong side of Circle C, placing stem through hole in plastic canvas. Overcast bottom edge of Base Band to Circle C. Insert 17¼"-wide corrugated cardboard against inside of Base Band; overlap short ends and glue. Stuff moderately. Overcast top edge of Base Band to Circle B.

5. Overcast one edge of Top Band to Circle D. Insert 9½"-wide corrugated cardboard against inside of Top Band; overlap short ends and glue. Stuff moderately. Overcast opposite edge of Top Band to Circle A.

6. Wrap mauve ribbon in and out through hole in bead until completely covered; glue end of ribbon to secure. Center and glue bead to top of Circle D. Space evenly and glue horses to top of Circle B.

7. Cut one 27" piece from mauve ribbon. Tie ribbon in a knot around bead, leaving even tails. Tie tails together 5½" from bead. Leaving knot on inner side of one horse's neck, tie a bow on outer side around neck. Repeat with light green ribbon and blue ribbon on other two horses.

8. Screw music box movement base to music box movement stem.

Codes

Stitch on clear Plastic Canvas 7 over one bar.

Pole (cut and stitch one, (see STEP 3 below)	34 x 34 bars
Top Band (cut and stitch one, (see STEP 3 below)	64 x 64 bars
Base Band (cut and stitch one)	18" x 4"
Heart (cut and stitch eleven)	4" x 4"

Stitch on clear Plastic Canvas 3" circles.

Circles A & D (cut and stitch one each, see STEP 4)	3" wide

Stitch on clear Plastic Canvas 6" circle.

Circles B & C (cut and stitch one each, see STEP 4)	5¼" wide

STEP 1: Continental stitch (twelve strands)

Skeins		DMC Floss	
3		224	Shell Pink-lt.
Skeins		**Watercolours** (three strands)	
5		007	Pistachio Nut

STEP 2: Long stitch (twelve strands)

Skeins		DMC Floss
1		3042 Antique Violet-lt. (Heart)

STEP 3: Long loose stitch (twelve strands)

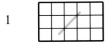

1	3041 Antique Violet-med. (Base Band)

STEP 4: Long stitch (eighteen strands). There are no graphs for the following pieces.

Pole—Using #503 floss, begin stitching two bars from left edge and three bars from top edge. Each stitch is placed diagonally two bars over and two bars up. When within two bars of edge, overlap ends of plastic canvas two bars to form a tube. Continue stitching to complete 32 stitches, securing overlap in stitches. For second row, select a new color as desired and repeat, making stitches which lie in the opposite direction. Repeat until Pole is completely stitched (see photo).

Top Band—Repeat above, overlapping ends and making two rows of 62 stitches using Antique Mauve-lt. only.

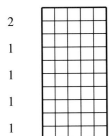

2	3727	Antique Mauve-lt.
1	316	Antique Mauve-med.
1	3041	Antique Violet-med.
1	932	Antique Blue-lt.
1	503	Blue Green-med.

STEP 5: Long stitch (three strands). There are no graphs for the following circles.

Circle A—Beginning one bar from outside edge, stitch over three bars toward center. Repeat around entire circle. Cut out center of circle, beginning one bar from stitched area.

Circle B—Beginning one bar from outside edge, stitch over eight bars toward center. Repeat around entire circle. Repeat, stitching over three more bars. Cut out center of circle, beginning one bar from stitched area.

Circle C—Beginning one bar from outside edge, stitch over 10 bars toward center. Repeat around entire circle. Cut out one bar at center.

Circle D—Beginning one bar from outside edge, stitch over six bars toward center. Repeat around entire circle. Stitch another circle over two remaining bars.

Watercolours

007   Pistachio Nut

STEP 6: Trim and overcast (six strands). When overcasting circles to bands, stitch around circle, then reverse direction and stitch again around circle.

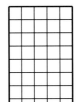

DMC Floss

3042   Antique Violet-lt. (Hearts)

Watercolours (three strands)

007   Pistachio Nut (all else)

STEP 7: Glue Hearts

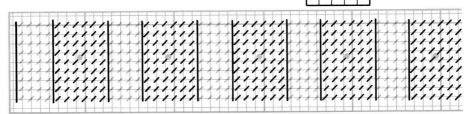

Base Band
Stitch Count: 111 x 11
Continue stitching designs to equal 111 x 11

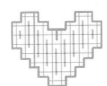

Heart
Stitch Count: 10 x 8

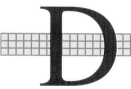 D is for the desk mates with a very macho flair,
And a frame for Billy Joe as he sits upon his mare.
Pencil holder, calendar frame—what more could you have asked?
They surely help the bossman at his daily working task!

Dynamic Desk Set

Finished sizes:
Calendar Holder—28½" W x 17½" H
Picture Frame—9½" W x 7⅜" H
Pencil Holder—4½" W x 6" H

Materials for Calendar Holder

Materials for stitching (see Codes)
1 (28½" x 17½") piece of unstitched clear
   Plastic Canvas 10 (Back)
1 (16½" x 24") calendar pad
Glue gun and glue

Directions

1. Stitch and trim plastic canvas pieces as directed in Codes.

2. Overcast turquoise edge of one Calendar Holder to one short edge of unstitched Back. Repeat on opposite side of Back. Using #530 Paternayan yarn, overcast remaining edges of Back.

3. Tack the inside edges of each Calendar Holder to Back piece, ¾" in from each Blue Spruce edge.

Materials for Pencil Holder

Materials for stitching (see Codes)
1 unstitched plastic canvas 4½" circle
1 (16 oz.) can

Directions

1. Stitch and trim plastic canvas pieces as directed in Codes.

2. Trim unstitched plastic canvas circle to 3¼"-diameter (Bottom).

3. Overcast short edges of Pencil Holder together to form a tube. Overcast Bottom to bottom edge of tube. Overcast top edge of Pencil Holder. Insert can.

Materials for Picture Frame

Materials for stitching (see Codes)
1 (18" x 14") piece of matte board
4" of ¼"-wide cream silk ribbon
   (see Suppliers)
Glue gun and glue
Craft knife

Directions

1. Stitch and trim plastic canvas pieces as directed in Codes.

2. Overcast inner and outer edges of frame.

3. To make back of frame, outline outer edge only of stitched Frame to make a pattern. Cut out pattern, omitting ⅛" from outer edges (Back). Using craft knife, cut one Back from matte board. Also from matte board, cut one 3" x 4½" piece (Stand). Mark a score line ¾" from one 3" edge of Stand. Fold along score line.

   With wrong side down and bottom edges aligned, center and glue top of Stand (above scored line) to Back. Place one end of ribbon 1" from bottom edge of Back and centered horizontally; glue. Glue other end of ribbon to wrong side of stand.

4. Center and glue Back to Frame, leaving one edge open. Allow to dry. Insert and center picture through open edge.

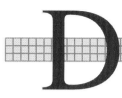

Codes

Stitch on clear Plastic Canvas 10 over one bar.

	Cut Size
Calendar Holder (cut and stitch two)	6" x 20"
Pencil Holder (cut and stitch one)	12" x 8"
Frame (cut and stitch one)	11" x 9"

STEP 1: Continental stitch (two strands)

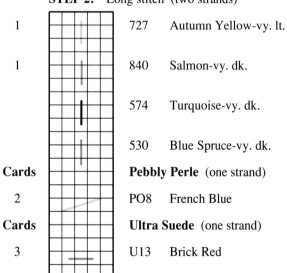

Skeins		Paternayan Persian Yarn
13		574 Turquoise-vy. dk.
16		530 Blue Spruce-vy. dk.
17		498 Wicker Brown-lt.

STEP 2: Long stitch (two strands)

1	727	Autumn Yellow-vy. lt.
1	840	Salmon-vy. dk.
	574	Turquoise-vy. dk.
	530	Blue Spruce-vy. dk.
Cards	**Pebbly Perle** (one strand)	
2	PO8	French Blue
Cards	**Ultra Suede** (one strand)	
3	U13	Brick Red

STEP 3: Couching (one strand)

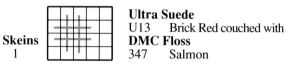

Skeins	**Ultra Suede**
1	U13 Brick Red couched with
	DMC Floss
	347 Salmon

STEP 4: Trim and overcast (two strands)

Paternayan Persian Yarn

574	Turquoise-vy. dk. (Calendar Holder, see Step 2 of Directions; Pencil Holder, see Step 3 of Directions)
530	Blue Spruce-vy. dk. (Blue Spruce edge of Calendar Holder; Calendar Holder Back, see Step 2 of Directions; top edge of Pencil Holder; all edges of Picture Frame)

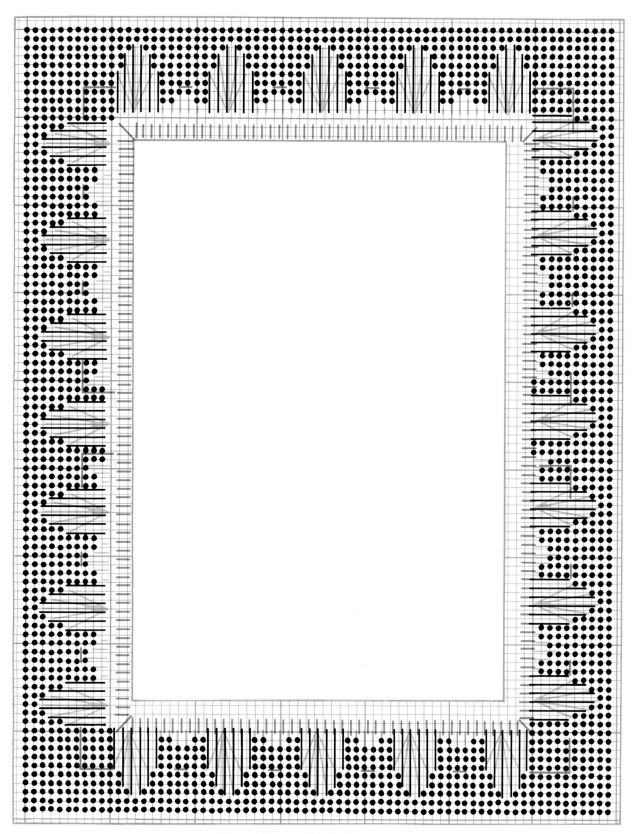

Picture Frame, Stitch Count: 36 x 178

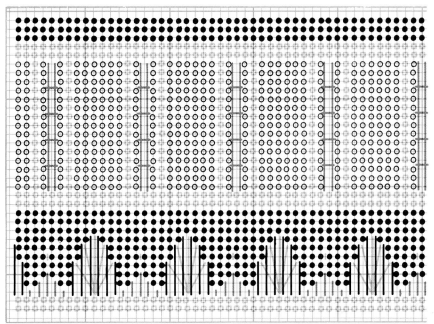

Pencil Holder
Stitch Count: 98 x 53
Continue stitching motifs until
stitch count equals 98 x 53.

Calendar Holder
Stitch Count: 36 x 178
Continue stitching motifs until
stitch count equals 36 x 178.

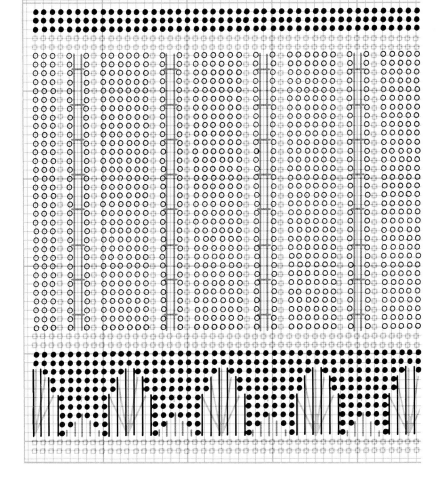

E is for Easter, and the flowers, and the spring,
And a basket that will cause any mother's heart to sing.
It is lovely when you fill if from the bottom to the brim,
With treasures such as daisies or Grandma's old lace trim.

Easter Ecstasy

Finished sizes:
Lavender and light pink flowers—3" W x 5" H
Dark pink flowers— 5" W x 5" H
Basket—9" W x 13" H

Materials

Materials for stitching (see Codes)
Scraps of fabric: light pink, salmon,
    lavender, dark pink, and dark green
8 (1" x ¾") pieces of unstitched clear
    Plastic Canvas 7
2½ yards of ½"-wide satin ribbon
1 dozen assorted silk flowers and
    leaves
Alene's Porcelain-ize-it (see Suppliers)
Assorted acrylic paints
High gloss varnish
1 (9" x 13") basket
Glue gun and glue

Directions

1. Stitch and trim plastic canvas pieces according to Codes.

2. Using one stitched Light Pink Petal, outline to make a pattern for Back. Repeat with stitched Small Dark Pink Petal, Large Dark Pink Petal and Leaf. From matching fabric, cut one Back for each corresponding petal and leaf, adding ¼" to entire edge. Fold one Back ¼" to wrong side and tack to back of corresponding petal. Repeat for remaining petals and leaves.

3. To make one light pink flower, arrange and tack six Light Pink Petals and three Light Green Leaves to one 1" x ¾" piece of unstitched plastic canvas. Repeat to make two light pink flowers.

4. To make remaining flowers, repeat Step 3, using the following per flower:

Salmon	Five Salmon Petals One Light Green Leaf
Lavender	Six Lavender Petals Two Dark Green Leaves
Dark pink	Five Large Dark Pink Petals Three Small Dark Pink Petals Two Light Green Leaves

5. Paint basket as desired. Allow to dry. Apply varnish. Paint and porcelainize ribbon and silk flowers as desired, following manufacturer's instructions.

6. Glue plastic canvas flowers, porcelainized flowers and ribbon as desired to basket

Codes

LEAVES

Stitch on clear Plastic Canvas 10 over one bar. The cut size for each leaf is 3" x 5". Cut and stitch twelve Light Green Leaves and four Dark Green Leaves.

STEP 1: Cross-stitch Light Green Leaf (six strands)

Skeins		DMC Floss	
2		3364	Pine Green
4		3363	Pine Green-med.

STEP 2: Cross-stitch Dark Green Leaf (six strands)

2		3363	Pine Green-med.
3		501	Blue Green-dk.

STEP 3: Trim and overcast (six strands)

		3364	Pine Green (Light Green Leaves)
		501	Blue green-dk. (Dark Green Leaves)

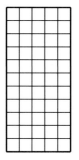

PETALS

Light pink and salmon flowers: Stitch on clear Plastic Canvas 10 over one bar. The cut size for each petal is 4" x 4". Cut and stitch 12 Light Pink Petals and 10 Salmon Petals.

Lavender flowers: Stitch on clear Plastic Canvas 10 over one bar. The cut size for each petal is 4" x 4". Cut and stitch 16 Lavender Petals.

Dark pink flowers: Stitch on clear Plastic Canvas 10 over one bar. The cut size for each small petal is 4" x 4". The cut size for each large petal is 4" x 5". Cut and stitch 6 Small Dark Pink Petals and 10 Large Dark Pink Petals.

STEP 1: Cross-stitch Light Pink Petal (six strands):

Skeins		DMC Floss	
2		818	Baby Pink
4		224	Shell Pink-lt.
1		3716	Wild Rose-lt.
1		3688	Mauve-med.

STEP 2: Cross-stitch Salmon Petal (six strands)

3		3708	Melon-lt.
1		776	Pink-med.
2		962	Wild Rose-med.
1		3350	Dusty Rose-dk.

STEP 3: Cross-stitch Lavender Petal (six strands)

Skeins		DMC Floss	
3		211	Lavender-lt.
2		3747	Blue Violet-vy. lt.
1		341	Blue Violet-lt.
1		340	Blue Violet-med.
1		3363	Pine Green-med.

STEP 4: Cross-stitch Small Dark Pink Petal and Large Dark Pink Petal (six strands):

2		3708	Melon-lt.
5		962	Wild Rose-med.
		3350	Dusty Rose-dk.

Skeins

5		3350	Dusty Rose-dk.
2		3363	Pine Green-med.

STEP 5: Trim and overcast (six strands)

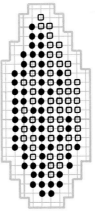

	211	Lavender-lt. (Lavender Petals)
	962	Wild Rose-med. (all Dark Pink Petals)
	3716	Wild Rose-lt. (Light Pink Petals)
	3708	Melon-lt. (Salmon Petals)

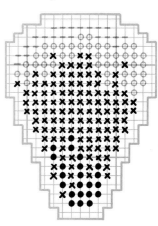

Dark Green Leaf
Light Green Leaf
Stitch Count: 10 x 22

Large Dark Pink Petal
Stitch Count: 17 x 22

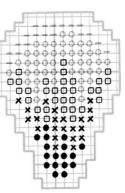

Lavendar Petal
Small Dark Pink Petal
Stitch Count: 14 x 19

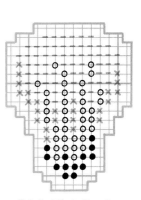

Light Pink Petal
Salmon Petal
Stitch Count: 14 x 18

F is for fruit in a basket made for fun,
And it doesn't even spoil in the golden noonday sun.
It is a perfect center piece when the season it is over.
You can pretend the snow is simply green and filled with clover.

Fun Fruit

Finished sizes:

Pear—4" W x 6" H
Apple—3" W x 3" H
Nectarine—2" W x 2" H
Grapes —4" W x 8" H

Materials

Materials for stitching (see Codes)
1 (1"-long) branch for apple stem
1 skein of #327 DMC floss
1 skein of #319 DMC floss
Stuffing
7 green floral wires (available at
    floral shop)
⅛"-wide dowel
Glue gun and glue

Directions

1. Stitch and trim plastic canvas pieces as directed in Codes.

2. To make one pear, overcast straight edges of stitched Pear together to form a tube. Using the floss that best matches adjacent stitching, whipstitch bottom edges closed (Diagram 1). Stuff moderately. Whipstitch top edges closed. Whipstitch Pear Leaves to top of pear (see photo).

Diagram 1

3. To make nectarine and apple, repeat Step 2 above, whipstitching one Nectarine Leaf only to each nectarine. Glue branch to center of apple leaves.

4. To make grapes, repeat Step 2, omitting leaves. Using six strands of #327 floss, thread through violet end of each grape to form a bunch, leaving long tails of floss. Pull all tails to top of bunch. Tightly wrap #319 floss around tails to form a ¼"-diameter x 1½"-high stem, placing small amounts of glue along stem as you wrap to secure floss (see photo). Tuck the ends of the floss under and glue. To make vines, wrap floral wire around dowel to make a 1"-long coil. Repeat to make six additional vines. Glue vines as desired to bunch. Glue grapes to each other as needed to keep bunch stationary. Tack grape leaf at bottom of stem.

Codes

Stitched on clear Plastic Canvas 10 over one bar.

	Cut Size
Pear Leaf (cut and stitch two)	4" x 6"
Nectarine Leaf (cut and stitch two)	4" x 4"
Apple Leaf (cut and stitch two)	3" x 5"
Grape Leaf (cut and stitch one)	6" x 6"
Pear (cut and stitch one)	12" x 9"
Nectarine (cut and stitch two)	9" x 6"
Apple (cut and stitch one)	11" x 7"
Grape (cut and stitch 20)	6" x 4"

STEP 1: Cross-stitch all leaves (six strands)

Skeins		DMC Floss	
4	–	772	Pine Green-lt.
2	⊙	3364	Pine Green
2		3363	Pine Green-med.
1		319	Pistachio Green-vy. dk.

STEP 2: Cross-stitch Pear (six strands)

Skeins		DMC Floss	
8		3078	Golden Yellow-vy. lt.

Codes continued on next page

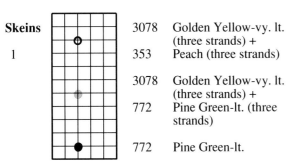

Skeins		DMC Floss	
1	⊕	3078	Golden Yellow-vy. lt. (three strands) +
		353	Peach (three strands)
		3078	Golden Yellow-vy. lt. (three strands) +
	●	772	Pine Green-lt. (three strands)
	●	772	Pine Green-lt.

STEP 3: Cross-stitch Nectarine (six strands)

Skeins		DMC Floss	
1	⊞	772	Orange Spice-lt.
2	○	352	Coral-lt.
2	●	3712	Salmon-med.

STEP 4: Cross-stitch Apple (six strands)

Skeins		DMC Floss	
1	–	350	Coral-med.
3	⊙	817	Coral Red-vy. dk.
3	○	498	Christmas Red-dk.
2	●	815	Garnet-med.

STEP 5: Cross-stitch Grape (six strands)

Skeins		DMC Floss	
6	⊙	3350	Dusty Rose-dk.
7	■	3685	Mauve-dk.
4	○	327	Antique Violet-vy. dk.

STEP 6: Trim and overcast (six strands). Select floss that best matches adjacent stitching (see Directions).

498	Christmas Red-dk.
815	Garnet-med.
352	Coral-lt.
3712	Salmon-med.
3350	Dusty Rose-dk.

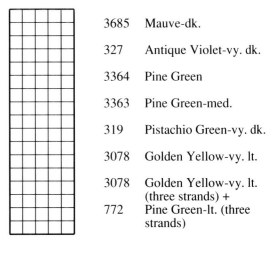

3685	Mauve-dk.
327	Antique Violet-vy. dk.
3364	Pine Green
3363	Pine Green-med.
319	Pistachio Green-vy. dk.
3078	Golden Yellow-vy. lt.
3078	Golden Yellow-vy. lt. (three strands) +
772	Pine Green-lt. (three strands)

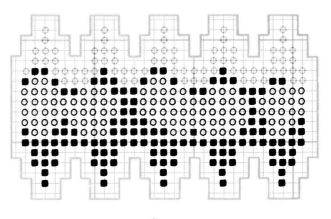

Grape
Stitch Count: 31 x 18

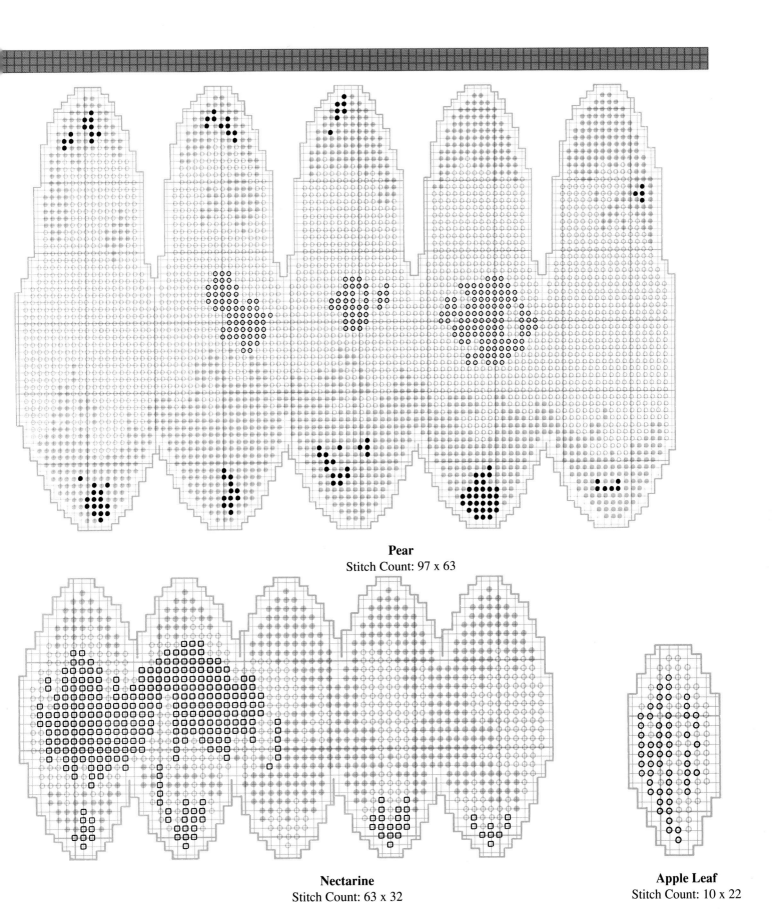

Pear
Stitch Count: 97 x 63

Nectarine
Stitch Count: 63 x 32

Apple Leaf
Stitch Count: 10 x 22

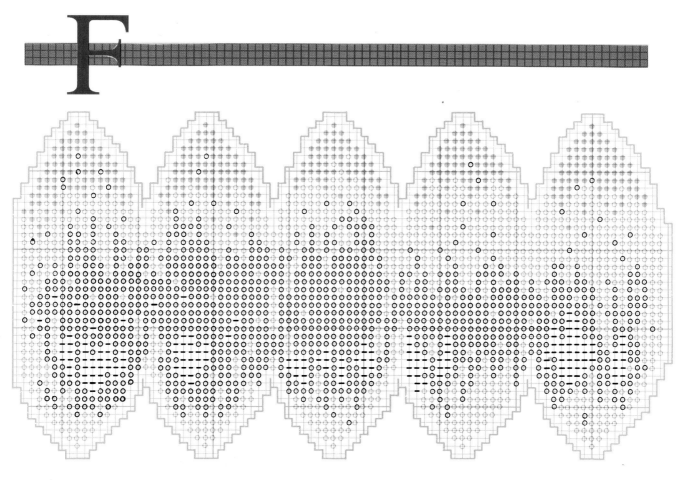

Apple
Stitch Count: 87 x 44

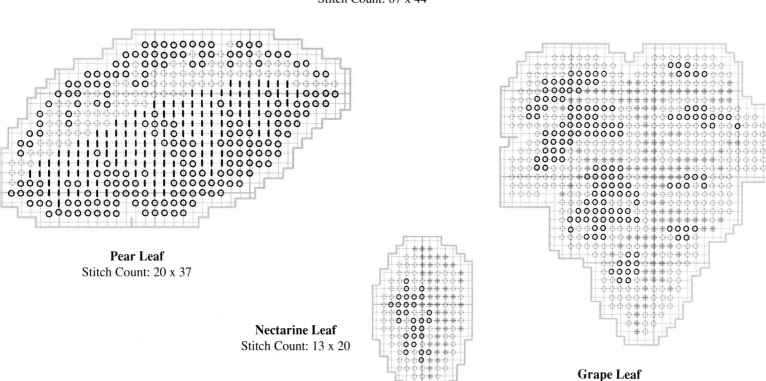

Pear Leaf
Stitch Count: 20 x 37

Nectarine Leaf
Stitch Count: 13 x 20

Grape Leaf
Stitch Count: 33 x 35

G is for gazebo and the most musical of geese,
Two very special gifts that are guaranteed to please,
A very loving mother, a sister or an aunt,
Who'd rather get these than the same old green house plant.

Garden Gazebo

Finished size: 9" W x 10" H x 9" D

Materials

Materials for stitching (see Codes)
French ribbon*
  4 yards of ¾"-wide lavender
  2¼ yards of ¾"-wide light blue
  7½ yards of ½"-wide lavender/blue
  2¾ yards of ½"-wide green
1 yard of ¹⁄₁₆"-wide lilac grosgrain ribbon*
Setacolor paints*: Cobalt Blue, Oriental Red, Black Lake
Two small plastic spray bottles
Glue gun and glue
*see Suppliers

Directions

1. Stitch and trim plastic canvas pieces as directed in Codes.

2. Overcast inner edges of Section C. Overcast long edges of all Section Cs together to make an open octagon. Overcast angled edges of Section Bs together to make roof. Overcast angled edges of Section As together to make steeple.

3. Overcast steeple to top of roof. Then overcast open box to roof. Overcast Section D to bottom of open box with the stitching facing inside.

4. To paint gazebo, mix blue with a drop of black Setacolor in one spray bottle. Repeat with red and black. Lightly spray paint gazebo (see photo).

5. Make nine large roses from lavender ribbon and 20 large carnations from light blue ribbons. Center and glue one rose on each Section B of lid. Glue three large carnations

at a 45° angle on one Section C (this will be the front of the gazebo). Glue remaining large carnations around rose on each Section B (see photo).

6. To make rose buds, cut a 2" piece of lavender/blue ribbon. Roll ribbon to form bud; secure ends with thread. Repeat to make 130 additional buds. Set aside.

7. Cut one 16" and one 11" piece from grosgrain ribbon. Wrap 16" piece around top edge of gazebo where lid and steeple meet; tie a bow in front. Tie 11" piece in a bow; center and glue ⅛" below first bow. Curl ribbon tails. Glue 14 rose buds in a bouquet over knots in bows (see photo). Glue remaining rose buds as desired around large rose and carnations.

8. Make 46 leaves from green ribbons. Glue as desired around all flower bouquets on gazebo (see photo).

Codes

Stitch on clear Plastic Canvas 7 over one bar.

	Cut Size
Section A (cut and stitch three)	4" x 4"
Section B (cut and stitch eight)	5" x 6"
Section C (cut and stitch eight)	5" x 8"
Section D (cut and stitch one)	9" x 9"

STEP 1: Continental stitch (one strand)

Skeins		Windrush Yarn
1		White
Cards		**Estaz** (two strands)
4		01 Pearl
Spools		**Balger #32 (heavy) Braid**
1		032 Pearl

STEP 2: Long stitch (one strand)

Windrush Yarn

White

White

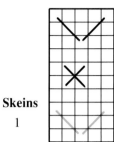

Sew Your Wild Threads

Skeins

1   907   Strip

STEP 3: Rhodes stitch (one strand)

Balger #32 (heavy) Braid

032   Pearl

STEP 4: Trim and overcast (one strand)

Windrush Yarn

White (see Step 2 of Directions)

Section A, Stitch Count: 10 x 14

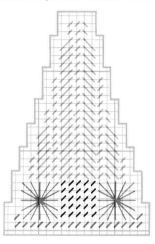

Section B, Stitch Count: 19 x 28

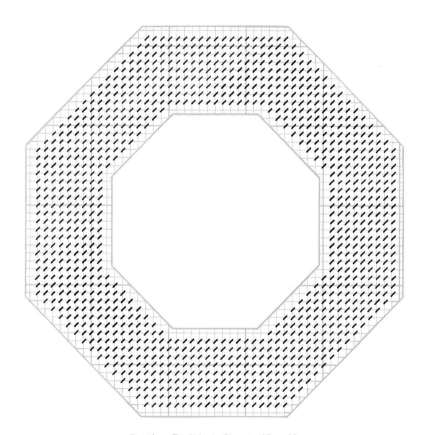

Section D, Stitch Count: 49 x 49

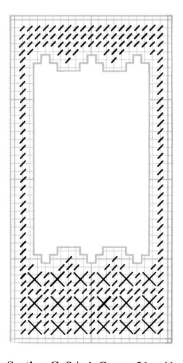

Section C, Stitch Count: 21 x 41

Gaggle of Geese

Finished size: 5½" W x 10½" H x 5½" D

Materials

Materials for stitching (see Codes)
1 yard of ¼"-wide light blue velvet ribbon
½ yard of ¾"-wide white scalloped trim
¾ yard of ¹⁄₁₆"-wide light blue satin ribbon
4 (3"-high) white flocked geese (available at craft stores)
1 (1⅜"-diameter) wood bead
1 (17¼" x 1¼") piece of corrugated cardboard
1 (9½" x ⅝") piece of corrugated cardboard
Music box movement #572 (see Suppliers)
Stuffing
White acrylic paint
Glue gun and glue

Directions

1. Stitch and trim plastic canvas pieces as directed in Codes.

2. Construct carousel following Steps 3-5 of *Carousel Fantasy* (pg. 26).

3. Paint bead white; allow to dry. Center and glue to top of Circle A. Cut one 10½" and one 6" piece of scalloped trim. Center and glue 10½" piece around Top Band. Center and glue 6" piece around pole. Space evenly and glue geese to top of Circle C.

4. Cut four 6" pieces from satin ribbon. Glue one end of each piece to the inner side of each goose's neck. Glue other end on the diagonal to Circle D (see photo). Cut velvet ribbon into four equal pieces. Tie one piece in a bow around the neck of each goose.

5. Screw music box movement base to music box movement stem. Glue Hearts at each ● (see graph).

Codes

Stitch on clear Plastic Canvas 7 over one bar. The graphs for the Base Band and Heart are on page 27.

	Cut Size
Pole (cut and stitch one)	7" x 7"
Top Band (cut and stitch one)	12" x 3
Base Band (cut and stitch one)	18" x 4"
Heart (cut and stitch eleven)	4" x 4"

Stitch on clear Plastic Canvas 3" circles (see Suppliers).

Circles A & D   3"
(cut and stitch one each, see STEP 4 below)

Stitch on clear Plastic Canvas 6" circles (see Suppliers).

Circles B & C   5¼"
(cut and stitch one each, see STEP 4 below)

STEP 1: Continental stitch (one strand)

Skeins		Windrush Yarn
1	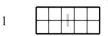	90200 Snow
1		90111 Powder Blue-lt.

STEP 2: Long stitch (one strand)

1		9015 Pink Heather (Heart)

STEP 3: Long loose stitch (one strand)

 90111 Powder blue-lt. (Base Band)

STEP 4: Long stitch (one strand). See STEP 4 of *Carousel Fantasy*, pg. 27. Only one color is used.

9011 Powder Blue (Top Band and Pole)

STEP 5: Long stitch (one strand). See STEP 5 of *Carousel Fantasy*, pg. 27.

9011 Powder Blue

STEP 6: Trim and overcast (one strand)

 9015 Pink Heather (Hearts)

9011 Powder Blue (all else)

H is for these special hearts, not just a valentine.
Tie them to your door or hand them from a vine.
Use them in the spring and all the winter through,
To tell your family that your love for them is always true.

∎ Heart-Felt Valentines ∎

Finished sizes:
Cut-out Heart—6" W x 4½" H x 1½" D
Pocket Heart—7" W x 6½" H x 1½" D

Materials for Cut-out Heart

Materials for stitching (see Codes)
½ yard of ½"-wide mauve satin ribbon;
    matching thread
¼ yard of ½"-wide light pink satin ribbon;
    matching thread
¾ yard each of ⅛"-wide mauve, light pink
    and light green silk ribbon*
2 yards of ⅛"-wide burgundy silk ribbon*
Tacky glue
*see Suppliers

Directions

1. Stitch and trim plastic canvas pieces as directed in Codes.

2. Center and whipstitch Tab to back of Heart E. Center and whipstitch Tab/Heart E to front of Back B.

3. Whipstitch Half Hearts together on short edges. Tack to front of Back B, matching cleavages and bottom points (see photo).

4. Make one large carnation using ½"-wide light pink ribbon (see General Instructions). Make four large carnations using mauve ribbon. Make 16 small carnations using burgundy ribbon. Glue flowers as desired to right half of Heart E (see photo).

5. To make leaves, cut nine 1" pieces from light green ribbon. Loop and glue as desired on bouquet of flowers (see photo).

6. Cut two 10" pieces from ⅛"-wide mauve, light-pink, and burgundy ribbons. Handling all ribbons as one, tie in a bow. Tack to cleavage of Back B (see photo).

Materials for Pocket Heart

Materials for stitching (see Codes)
3¼ yards of ⅛"-wide dark mauve silk ribbon*
1 yard of ⅛"-wide burgundy silk ribbon*
½ yard of ⅛"-wide light green silk ribbon*
½ yard of ½"-wide pink satin ribbon
*see Suppliers

Directions

1. Stitch and trim plastic canvas pieces as directed in Codes.

2. Whipstitch Pocket to right side of Back A, matching each corner with each ● (see graph).

3. Make four large carnations with mauve ribbon. Make 10 small carnations with burgundy ribbon. Glue as desired on lower right edge of Pocket (see photo). To make leaves, cut 10 1" pieces from light green ribbon. Loop and glue as desired on bouquet of flowers.

4. Cut five 9" pieces from dark mauve ribbon. Thread one piece through cleavage of each medium and small heart. Tie each ribbon in a bow, then knot all ends. Tack remaining hearts as desired to front of Back A (see photo).

5. From dark mauve ribbon, cut one piece each of the following: 8", 18", 20" and 22". Thread 8" piece through cleavage of Back A and tie ends in a knot around center of remaining ribbons, leaving a 3½" loop for hanging. Handling ribbons as one, tie them in a bow.

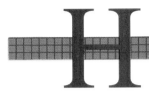

Codes

Stitch on white Plastic Canvas 7 over one bar.

	Cut Size
Pocket Heart	
Heart A (cut and stitch two)	4" x 4"
Heart B (cut and stitch one)	4" x 4"
Heart C ((cut and stitch one)	6" x 6"
Heart D (cut and stitch one)	6" x 6"
Pocket (cut and stitch one)	6" x 6"
Back A (cut and stitch one)	9" x 8"
Cut-out Heart	
Heart E (cut and stitch one)	6" x 5"
Half Heart (cut and stitch two)	5" x 7"
Back B (cut and stitch one)	8" x 7"
Tab (cut and stitch one)	3" x 3"

STEP 1: Continental stitch and reverse continental stitch (two strands)

Skeins		DMC Pearl Cotton #3	
4	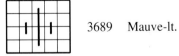	3689	Mauve-lt. (Back B, Heart D)
4		899	Rose-med. (Back A, Half Hearts, one Heart B)
2		309	Rose-deep (two Heart As, Heart C, Heart E)

STEP 2: Long stitch (two strands)

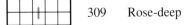

	3689	Mauve-lt. (Heart B, Heart D)
	309	Rose-deep (Heart C, Heart E)

STEP 3: Double Parisian stitch (two strands)

	3689	Mauve-lt.

STEP 4: Backstitch (one strand)

	309	Rose-deep

STEP 5: Trim and overcast (two strands)

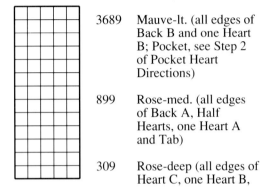

3689	Mauve-lt. (all edges of Back B and one Heart B; Pocket, see Step 2 of Pocket Heart Directions)
899	Rose-med. (all edges of Back A, Half Hearts, one Heart A and Tab)
309	Rose-deep (all edges of Heart C, one Heart B,

Tab, Stitch Count: 4 x 4

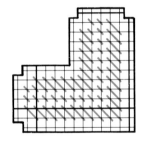

Heart C, Stitch Count: 13 x 13

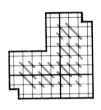

Heart A, Stitch Count: 9 x 9

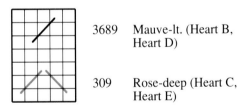

Heart B, Stitch Count: 9 x 9

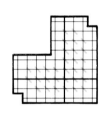

Heart D, Stitch Count: 13 x 13

Heart E, Stitch Count: 22 x 19

Pocket, Stitch Count: 23 x 23

Half Heart, Stitch Count: 20 x 30

Back B, Stitch Count: 40 x 30

Back A, Stitch Count: 44 x 38

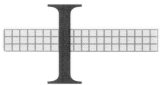

You cannot find a name and your recipe is gone,
You've looked high and low from dusk until dawn.
My friend, what is needed is quite easy to see,
An "Itsy Bitsy Index Box" is the answer—and its free!

Itsy Bitsy Index Box

Finished size: 5½" W x 4" H x 3⅛" D

Directions

1. Stitch and trim plastic canvas pieces as directed in Codes.

2. To make house, overcast Left Front Panel to Right Front Panel, using floss that matches adjacent stitching. Then overcast Left Back Panel to Right Back Panel, using ecru floss.

Place Door on front of house (see graph). Cross-stitch outside row of door through all plastic canvas layers to secure, using white floss.

Using #402 floss, overcast short edges of Left End Panel and Right End Panel to front and back sections to form an open box. Overcast top edges with #3046 floss. Overcast bottom edges with #989 floss.

3. To make inner box, cut matte board in the following pieces: two 5¼" x 3⅜" pieces, two 3" x 3⅜" pieces, and one 5⅜" x 3⅛" piece. Tape 5¼" x 3⅜" and 3" x 3⅜" pieces together to form an open box. Tape 5⅜" x 3⅛" to bottom of box. Glue inner box to inside of house.

4. To make roof, cut two Triangles from matte board. Then cut two 5⅝" x 1⅞" pieces and one 5⅝" x 3⅛" piece. Lay matte board pieces flat (Diagram 1). Tape all seams.

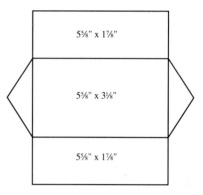

5⅝" x 1⅞"

5⅝" x 3⅛"

5⅝" x 1⅞"

Diagram 1

Fold all ends pieces up to form roof. Cover with brown paper.

Whipstitch Roofs together along one long edge. Glue matte board roof to inside of stitched roof. Place on top of house.

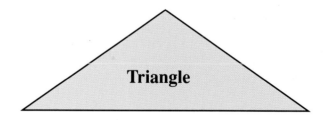

Triangle

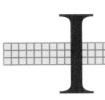

Codes

Stitch on cream Plastic Canvas 14 over one bar.

	Cut Size
Left Front Panel (cut and stitch one)	4" x 4"
Right Front Panel (cut and stitch one)	4" x 4"
Left Back Panel (cut and stitch one)	4" x 4"
Right Back Panel (cut and stitch one)	4" x 4"
Left End Panel (cut and stitch one)	4" x 4"
Right End Panel (cut and stitch one)	4" x 4"
Door (cut and stitch one)	5" x 7"

Stitch on light green Plastic Canvas 10 over one bar.

Roof (cut and stitch two)	8" x 5"

STEP 1: Cross-stitch (three strands)

Skeins		DMC Floss	
1	⊕		White
1	▲	3046	Yellow Beige-med.
1	●	402	Mahogany-vy. lt.
1	■	977	Golden Brown-lt.
1		221	Shell Pink-vy. dk.
1		498	Christmas Red-dk.
1		3042	Antique Violet-lt.
1		553	Violet-med.
1		828	Blue-ultra vy. lt.
1		368	Pistachio Green-lt.
1		367	Pistachio Green-dk.
1	✗	989	Forest Green
1		3348	Yellow Green-lt.
1		3345	Hunter Green-dk.
1		738	Tan-vy. lt
1	—	407	Pecan
1	✖	644	Beige Gray-med.
1	▲	640	Beige Gray-vy. dk.
1		414	Steel Gray-dk.

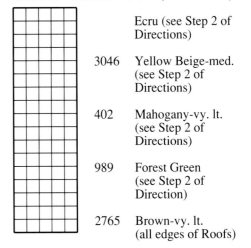

STEP 2: Woven stitch (one strand)

DMC Matte Cotton

1	2421	Hazel Nut Brown

STEP 3: Continental stitch (one strand)

DMC Matte Cotton

1	2765	Brown-vy. lt.

STEP 4: Backstitch (one strand)

DMC Floss

402	Mahogany-vy. lt. (right and left edges of front and sides)
989	Forest Green (two strands) (roof)
3345	Hunter Green-dk. (bushes)
407	Pecan (brick lines, windows on side sections, complete upper right window, left panel of lower right window)
640	Beige Gray-vy. dk. (all else)

STEP 5: Cut and overcast (three strands)

	Ecru (see Step 2 of Directions)
3046	Yellow Beige-med. (see Step 2 of Directions)
402	Mahogany-vy. lt. (see Step 2 of Directions)
989	Forest Green (see Step 2 of Direction)
2765	Brown-vy. lt. (all edges of Roofs)

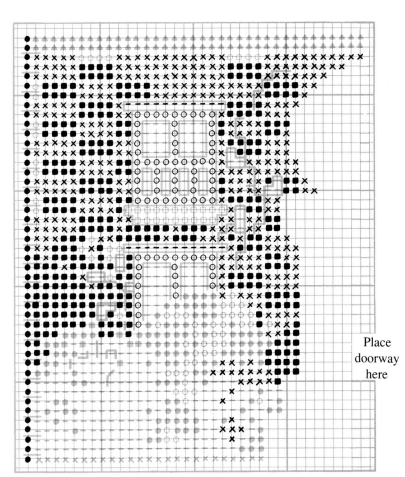

Left Front Panel
Stitch Count: 44 x 47

Place
doorway
here

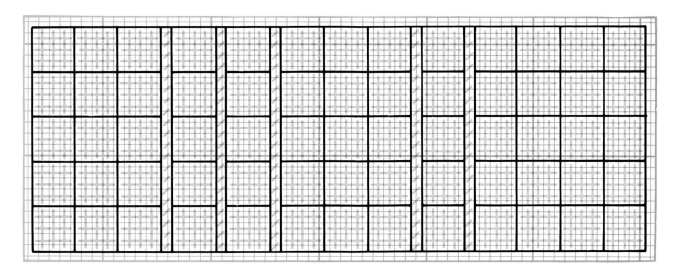

Roof
Stitch Count: 59 x 22

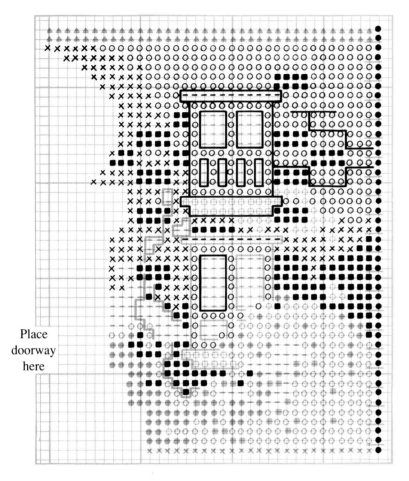

Right Front Panel
Stitch Count: 44 x 47

Place
doorway
here

Door
Stitch Count: 22 x 42

Left Back Panel
Stitch Count: 39 x 47

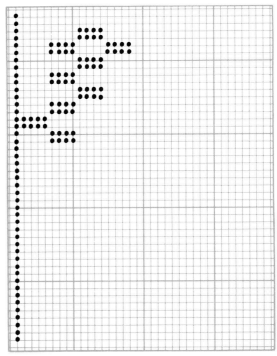

Left End Panel
Stitch Count: 24 x 44

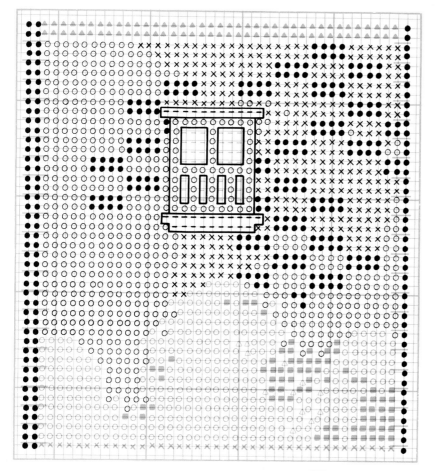

Right Back Panel
Stitch Count: 39 x 47

Right End Panel
Stitch Count: 24 x 44

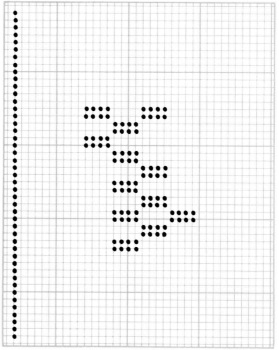

 **J** is for the jingle, or a jester, or just jack,
Who's such a happy fellow because we didn't name him Mack!
He sits upon your table happy the whole year through,
And sings a quiet lovely song made especially for you two.

Jingle Jack

Finished size: 5" W x 10" H x 5" D

Materials

Materials for stitching (see Codes)
2 (33 x 33 bar) pieces of clear
   unstitched plastic canvas
¾ yard of green satin; matching thread
½ yard of burgundy satin; matching thread
Scrap of muslin
Stuffing
Ceramic head (see Suppliers)
1 (50-mm) gold jingle bell
8 (½"-long) clear diamond faceted beads
8 (⅜"-long) clear diamond faceted beads
8 (⅜"-wide) gold ball beads
32 (1-mm) gold glass beads
8 (1-mm) clear glass beads
1 yard of monofilament
¾ cup of sand
Glue gun and glue

Directions

All seam allowances are ¼".

1. Stitch and trim plastic canvas pieces as directed in Codes.

2. To make sandbag, cut one 6½" x 3½" piece from muslin. Fold muslin in half to measure 3¼" wide. Stitch the sides, leaving the top open. Turn. Fill with sand. Slipstitch opening closed. Set aside.

3. To make box, overcast four Panels together to make an open box. Overcast one piece of unstitched plastic canvas to one open side of bottom of box. Stuff box ¼ full with stuffing. Insert sandbag. Stuff box firmly. Overcast remaining unstitched plastic canvas to top of box. Overcast remaining Panels together with wrong sides facing for lid.

Whipstitch one edge of lid to one edge at top of box.

4. From green satin, cut one Hat, four Collars and one 18" x 4" piece for Ruffle. From burgundy satin, cut two Collars, one 18" x 4" piece for Ruffle and one 1¾" x 22" piece for Hat Band.

5. With wrong sides facing and raw edges aligned, fold one Ruffle to measure 18" x 2". Stitch gathering threads on long raw edge. Repeat with remaining Ruffle. Set aside.

6. Stitch two burgundy Collars together, with right sides facing, leaving neck edge open. Clip inside points. Turn; press. Stitch gathering threads on raw edges. Repeat with remaining Collars. Attach beads as follows: ⅜"-wide diamond faceted beads with 3 gold glass beads on points of one green collar, ½"-wide diamond faceted beads with 1 clear glass bead on points of burgundy collar, gold ball beads with one gold glass bead on points of remaining green Collar. Set aside.

7. Fold hat with right sides together and long edges aligned; stitch, leaving an opening. Turn. Fold hat band with right sides facing and matching short ends. Stitch short ends. Refold with wrong sides facing and matching raw edges. With right sides facing and raw edges of hat and band aligned, stitch hat to band. Tack jingle bell to point on hat. Set hat aside.

8. Gather green Ruffle to fit tightly around neck of ceramic head; secure threads in holes on neck of ceramic head. Repeat with burgundy Ruffle, then with collars in the following order: green, burgundy, green. Thread a long piece of plastic wire through holes, leaving long tails. Thread tails through unstitched plastic canvas on box from top to bottom, then back up to top; secure. Glue neck to top of box. Glue hat to top of head.

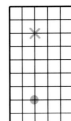

Codes

Stitch on clear Plastic Canvas 7 over one bar. The plastic canvas is cut 7" x 7". Cut and stitch six Panels.

STEP 1: Cross-stitch (one strand)

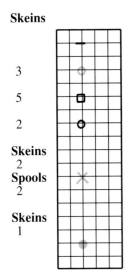

Skeins		DMC Pearl Cotton #3
		Ecru
3		598 Turquoise-lt.
5		991 Aquamarine-dk.
2		415 Pearl Gray

Skeins	DMC Pearl Cotton #3
2	3687 Mauve +
Spools	**Balger Blending Filament**
2	024 Fuchsia

Skeins	DMC Pearl Cotton #3
1	3685 Mauve-dk. +
	Balger Blending Filament
	024 Fuchsia (Balger)

Skeins		DMC Pearl Cotton #3
2		913 Nile Green-med. +
Spools		**Balger #16 Braid**
4		008 Green (Balger)
		DMC Pearl Cotton #3
		991 Aquamarine-dk. +
		Balger #16 Braid
		008 Green (Balger)

STEP 2: Scotch stitch (one strand)

3687	Mauve
598	Turquoise-lt.

STEP 3: Trim and overcast (one strand). See Step 3 of Directions.

	DMC Pearl Cotton #3
	991 Aquamarine-dk. +
	Balger #16 Braid
	008 Green (Balger)

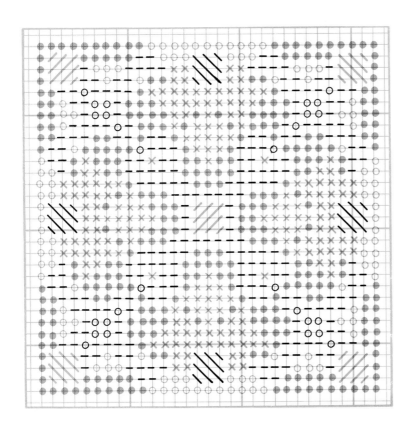

Panel
Stitch Count: 33 x 33

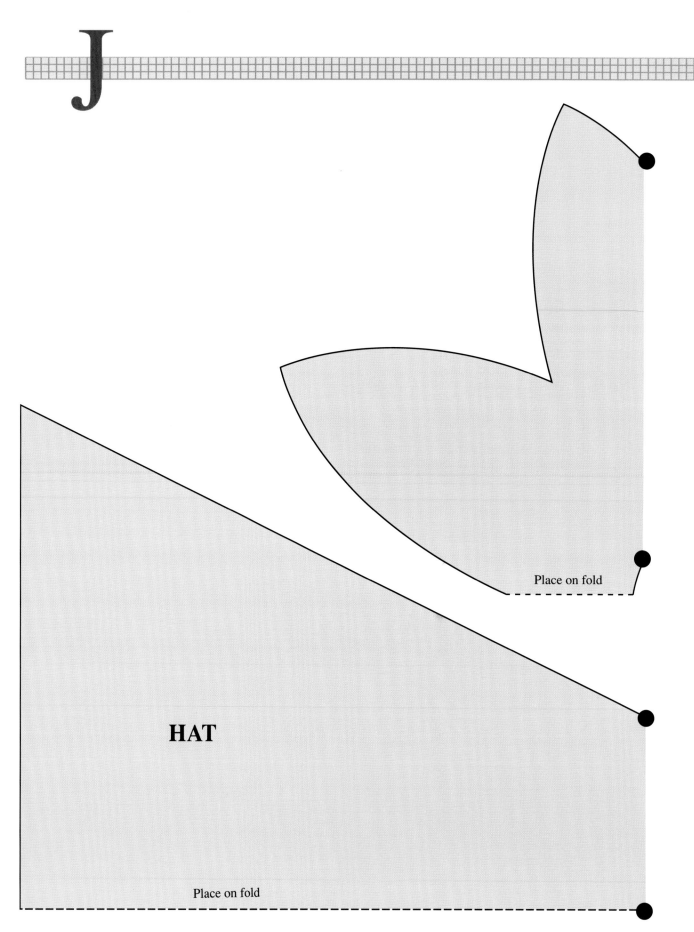

HAT

Place on fold

Place on fold

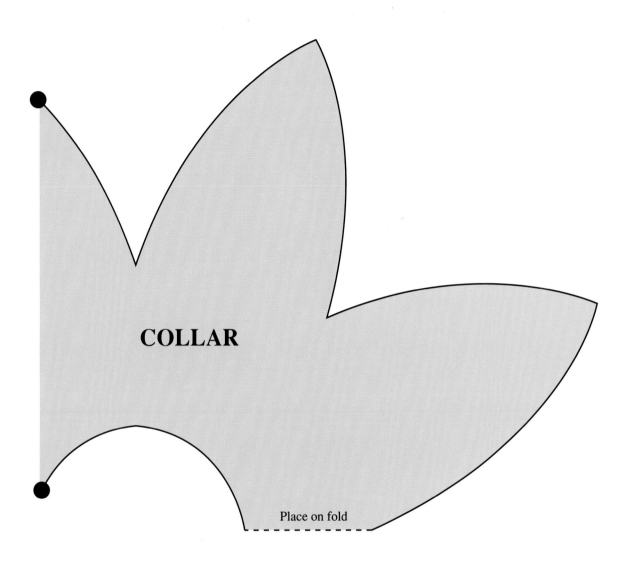

COLLAR

Place on fold

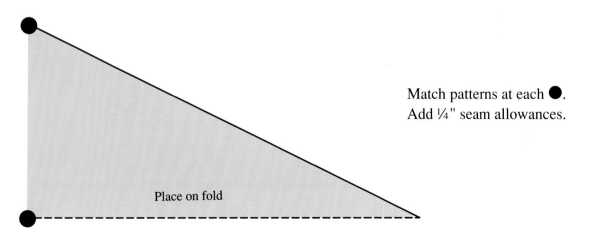

Match patterns at each ●.
Add ¼" seam allowances.

Place on fold

 **K** K is for kaleidoscope, need we say much more?
This wonderful invention is like a magical door.
Please turn it while you peek inside, what is it you do see?
A place that is as magical as magic it can be!

▪▦ Kaleidoscope Beauty ▦▪

Finished size: 21" W x 2¾" H x 2¾" D

Materials

Materials for stitching (see Codes)
2 (3") circles of unstitched plastic canvas *
1 yard of ⅜"-wide cream picot ribbon
1 yard of ¼"-wide light blue satin ribbon
1½ yards of ⅛"-wide light blue satin ribbon
1½ yards of ⅛"-wide dark blue satin ribbon
2 yards of ⅛"-wide mauve satin ribbon
50 (1-mm) glass beads each in 6 different
    colors*
10 (1-mm) glass beads of a different color
    than above*
Assorted blue and clear diamond faceted
    glass beads
1 (15" x 15") mirror (see Step 2 below)
1 (12" x 12") pane of thick glass (see Step 2)
Stripping tape
Super glue
*see Suppliers

Directions

1. Stitch and trim plastic canvas pieces as
   directed in Codes.

2. Have a professional cut two 2¼"-diameter
   circles and two 2½"-diameter circles cut
   from glass. Have edges sanded. Have three
   mirror pieces cut according to Mirror pattern. To make mirror tube, cut three 12"-
   long pieces of tape. Place mirror pieces
   parallel to each other and ¼" apart with
   wrong sides over two pieces of parallel tape
   (Diagram 1).

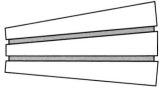

Diagram 1

Clean mirrors. Roll mirror pieces to form a
triangular tube with mirrors on inside.
Secure long edges with remaining piece of
tape. Then wrap additional tape around tube
to secure, leaving ends open. Be careful not
to smudge the mirrors.

3. To make plastic canvas tube, overcast long
   edges of Tube together. Clean 2¼" glass
   circles. Insert one glass circle to within ¼"
   of bottom end of plastic canvas tube (see
   graph for bottom). Overcast inner edge of
   Bottom, then overcast Bottom to bottom end
   of tube. Insert mirrors in tube with wide end
   facing top of tube. Position mirrors so that
   one flat edge is facing seam of tube. Insert
   remaining 2¼" glass circle to within ¼" of
   top of tube. Overcast inner edge of Eye
   Piece, then overcast Eye Piece to top of
   tube.

4. To make cap, overcast short edges of Band
   together. Overcast inner edge of Cap, then
   overcast Cap to Band.

   Cut two Wheels from unstitched plastic
   canvas. Glue Wheels together. Then carefully glue these to one 2½" glass circle.
   Insert the 10 1-mm beads in the center of the
   Wheels. Insert one color of the remaining 1-
   mm beads in each space of the wheel.
   Carefully glue remaining glass piece over
   top of wheel. Place in cap, pushing to
   bottom. Place cap on bottom of kaleidoscope.

5. Cut one 12" piece from one color of ribbon;
   thread through stitching at top side of kaleidoscope. Handling ribbons as one, tie in
   bow and secure to kaleidoscope with 12"
   piece. Trim ends. Thread diamond faceted
   beads as desired through tails of ribbons.
   Knot tails of ribbons.

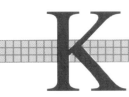

Codes

Stitch on clear Plastic Canvas 10 over one bar.

	Cut Size
Tube (cut and stitch one)	9" x 15"
Band (cut and stitch one)	10" x 4"

Stitch on clear Plastic Canvas 3" circles (see Suppliers).

	Cut Size
Eye Piece (cut and stitch one)	2¼"
Bottom (cut and stitch one)	2¼"
Cap (cut and stitch one)	2½"

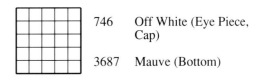

746	Off White (Eye Piece, Cap)
3687	Mauve (Bottom)

STEP 3: Trim and overcast (two strands)

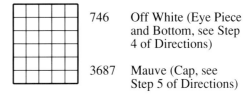

746	Off White (Eye Piece and Bottom, see Step 4 of Directions)
3687	Mauve (Cap, see Step 5 of Directions)

STEP 1: Continental stitch (one strand)

Skeins		DMC Pearl Cotton #3	
4	—	746	Off White
1	✕	745	Yellow-lt. pale
2	■	3687	Mauve
1	○	210	Lavender-med.
1	┼	800	Delft-pale
1	▢	813	Blue-lt.
1	●	924	Slate Green-vy. dk.
1	▣	320	Pistachio Green-med.
1	✳	762	Pearl Gray-vy. lt.

STEP 2: Long stitch on circles (two strands). Eye Piece—Beginning one bar from outside edge, stitch toward center over four bars. Repeat around entire circle. Cut out center of circle, beginning one bar from stitched area.

Bottom—Beginning one bar from outside edge, stitch toward center over three bars toward center. Repeat around entire circle. Cut out center of circle, beginning one bar from stitched area.

Cap—Beginning one bar from outside edge, stitch toward center over two bars. Repeat around entire circle. Cut out center of circle, beginning one bar from stitched area.

WHEEL

Match pattern
at each ●.

MIRROR

12³⁄₈"

1⅝"

¾"

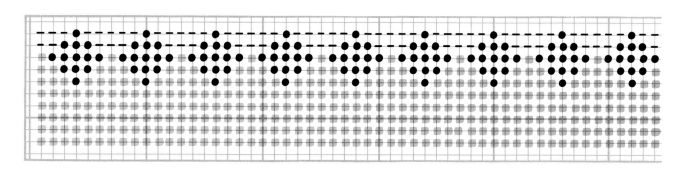

Band
Stitch Count: 75 x 12
Continue stitching motifs until stitch count equals 75 x 12

Tube
Stitch Count: 68 x 122

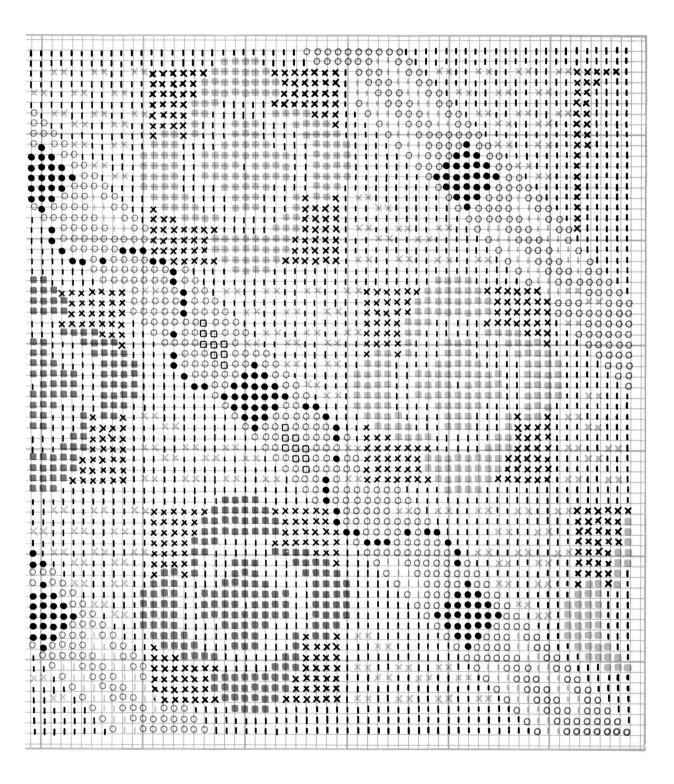

Bottom

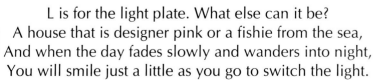 L is for the light plate. What else can it be?
A house that is designer pink or a fishie from the sea,
And when the day fades slowly and wanders into night,
You will smile just a little as you go to switch the light.

=▦▦Light 'em Up! ▦▦▦▦▦...

Finished sizes:
Fish—7" x 7"
House—6⅝" x 3⅞"

Materials (for one light-switch plate)

Materials for stitching (see Codes)
1 (8" x 8") piece of white cardboard
Craft knife
Glue gun and glue

Directions

1. Stitch and trim plastic canvas pieces as directed in Codes.

2. To make back of switch plate, outline trimmed design piece onto cardboard; cut out ⅛" inside outline. Glue cardboard to wrong side of design piece.

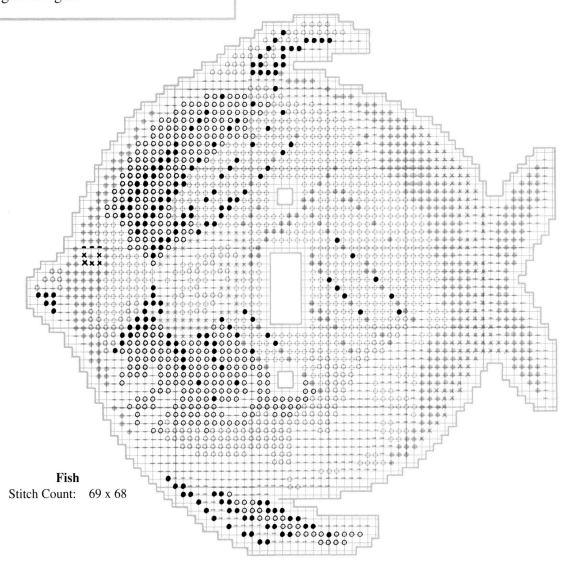

Fish
Stitch Count: 69 x 68

Codes

FISH SWITCH PLATE

Stitch on clear Plastic Canvas 10 over one bar. The plastic canvas is cut 9" x 9". Cut and stitch one.

STEP 1: Cross-stitch (four strands)

Skeins		DMC Floss	
2		745	Yellow-lt. pale
1		353	Peach
1		3326	Rose-lt.
1		211	Lavender-lt.
1		554	Violet-lt.
1		794	Cornflower Blue-lt.
2		793	Cornflower Blue-med.
1		791	Cornflower Blue-vy. dk.
1		964	Seagreen-lt.
1		562	Jade-med.
1		977	Golden Brown-lt.
1		976	Golden Brown med.

STEP 2: Trim and overcast

	793	Cornflower Blue-med.

HOUSE SWITCH PLATE

Stitch on clear Plastic Canvas 10 over one bar. The plastic canvas is cut 6" x 9". Cut and stitch one.

STEP 1: Cross-stitch (four strands)

Skeins		DMC Floss	
1		754	Peach-lt.
1		758	Terra Cotta-lt.
1		356	Terra Cotta-med.
1		760	Salmon
1		738	Tan-vy. lt.

STEP 2: Trim and overcast (four threads)

	754	Peach-lt. (match with adjacent stitching)
	758	Terra Cotta-lt. (match with adjacent stitching)
	356	Terra Cotta-med. (match with adjacent stitching)
	760	Salmon (match with adjacent stitching)
	738	Tan-vy. lt. (match with adjacent stitching)

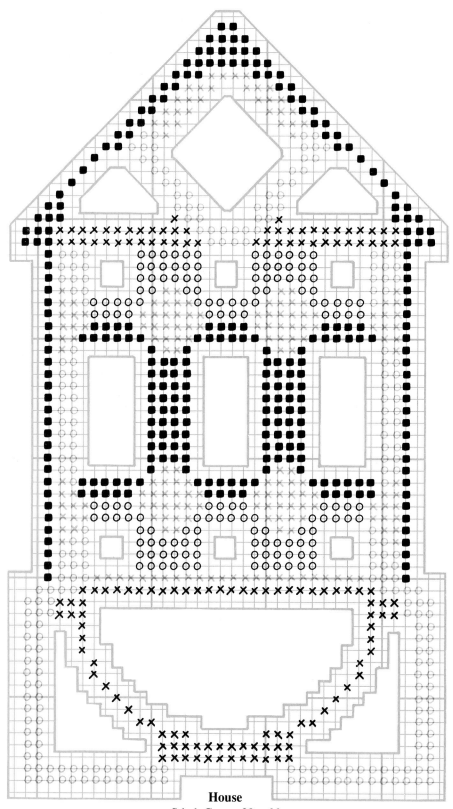

House
Stitch Count: 38 x 66

M is for a moon box, and it is plain to see,
That this box of many colors is as useful as can be.
Within a day or two you can stitch it up with ease,
It's a place to put your jewelry or your buttons or your keys.

Magical Moon

Finished size: 4½" W x 2" H x 5½" D

Codes

Stitch on clear Plastic Canvas 10 over one bar.

	Cut size
Lid (cut and stitch two)	7" x 8"
Bottom (cut and stitch two)	6" x 8"
Sides (see STEP 4 below):	
1 (cut and stitch one)	4" x 10"
2 (cut and stitch one)	4" x 14"
3 (cut and stitch one)	9" x 10"
4 (cut and stitch one)	9" x 15"

STEP 1: Continental stitch (one strand)

Cards   **Overture**

V43   Hacienda

STEP 2: Double cross-stitch (four strands). Stitch on one Lid only. Choose from the colors below at random.

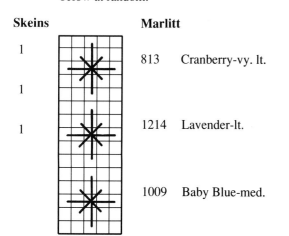

Skeins		Marlitt	
1		813	Cranberry-vy. lt.
1		1214	Lavender-lt.
1		1009	Baby Blue-med.

STEP 3: Glue faceted stones (on Lid with double cross-stitching only).

Stones		Stones (star shaped)
6		Clear
6		Blue

STEP 4: Continental stitch (one strand). Stitch Sides 1 through 4 as listed below. There are no graphs for these pieces.

Side 1—7 x 73 stitches
Side 2—7 x 128 stitches
Side 3—17 x 72 stitches
Side 4—17 x 120 stitches

Overture

V43   Hacienda

STEP 5: Trim and braid stitch (one strand)

V43   Hacienda (one long edge of all sides)

STEP 6: Overcast (two strands). With wrong sides of Lids facing, and with double cross-stitches on top, overcast edges of Sides 3 and 4 to edges of Lids, then overcast tips of sides together. Repeat with wrong sides of Bottoms. Place lid on box.

V43   Hacienda.

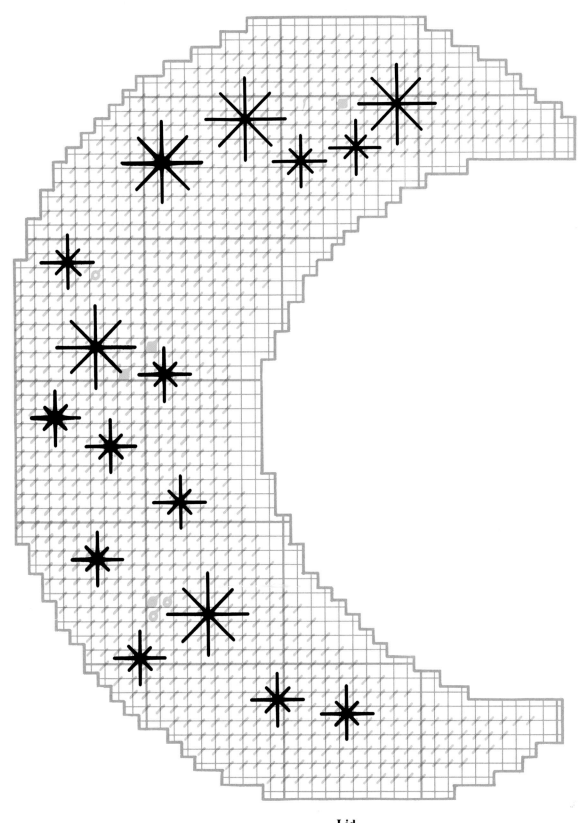

Lid
Stitch Count: 41 x 55

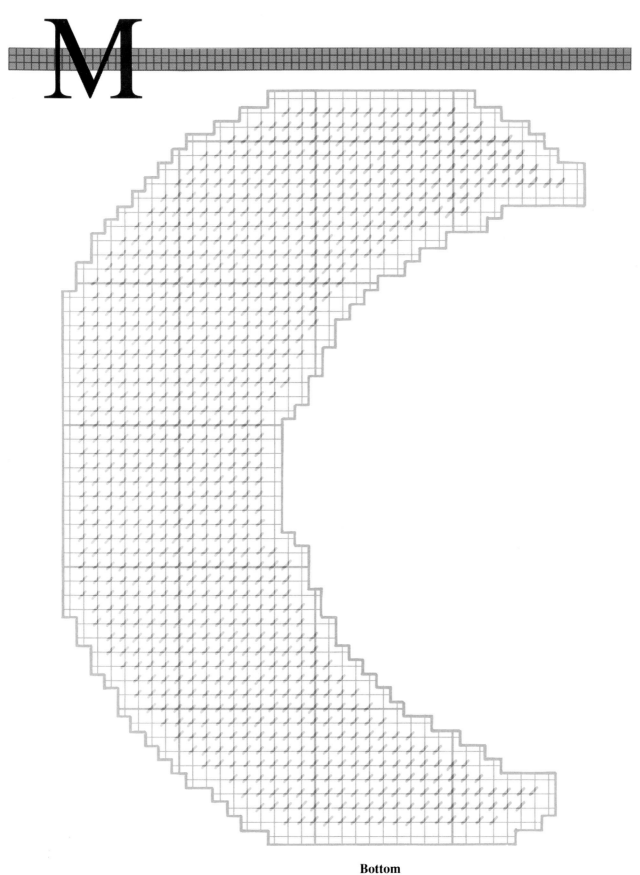

Bottom
Stitch Count: 38 x 53

 N is for my nutcrackers, a symbol for the year,
Announcing very loudly that it's Christmas time. It's here!
Designed for a collector or someone just like me,
Who loves to hang these little "men" all upon my tree.

Nutcracker Replicas

Finished size: 3" W x 7" H x 2" D

Materials

Materials for stitching (see Codes)
One package of Curly Roving
    (see Suppliers)
Glue gun and glue

Directions

1. Stitch and trim plastic canvas pieces as directed in Codes.

2. To make soldier, overcast short edges of Arms together, matching As and Bs, using Double Gold Metallic. Then overcast remaining edges of Arms, using floss that matches adjacent stitching. Whipstitch Arms to Body three bars from top of red shirt and seven bars from gold beads.

Overcast long edges of Body together, using floss that matches adjacent stitching. Overcast bottom edges of Body together (Diagram 1).

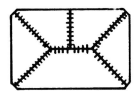

Diagram 1

Whipstitch top points of hat together (see photo). Whipstitch points of head together.

Glue roving on head for hair, and above and below lip for mustache and beard.

3. To make Santa, overcast short edges of Arms together, matching As and Bs, using

#321 floss. Then overcast remaining edges of Arms, using floss that matches adjacent stitching. Whipstitch Arms to Body three bars below top of red shirt and seven bars from the gold trim.

Overcast long edges of Body, bottom edges of Body and points of head and hat (see Step 2 above).

4. To make hangers for both nutcrackers, braid a 10" piece of thread to match hat. Thread ends through two sides on top of head; knot ends. Place hat on head, threading hanger through hole in top of hat (hat will be loose).

Codes

SOLDIER

Stitch on clear Plastic Canvas 10 over one bar.

	Cut size
Soldier Hat (cut and stitch one)	9" x 5"
Soldier Arm (cut and stitch two)	4" x 5
Soldier Body (cut and stitch one)	8" x 9"

STEP 1: Cross-stitch (one strand)

Skeins		DMC Pearl Cotton #5
1	−	White
1	⊕	754 Peach-lt.
1	✗	760 Salmon
1		321 Christmas Red
1		799 Delft-med.
1		798 Delft-dk.
1	●	310 Black

STEP 2: Half cross-stitch (one strand)

Cards		Double Gold Metallic
1		DG2C Gold

STEP 3: Long stitch (one strand)

		DG2C Gold (on Hat and boots, loops on Hat)
Spool		**Lamé Thread**
1		Gold (on jacket)

STEP 4: Backstitch (one strand)

Skeins		DMC Floss	
1		347	Salmon-vy. dk. (mouth)
1		435	Brown-vy. lt. (eyes, nose)

STEP 5: Beadwork

Beads		Beads	
12		02011	Victorian Gold

STEP 6: Trim and overcast (one strand). See Step 2 of Directions.

DMC Pearl Cotton #5

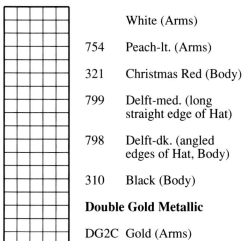

	White (Arms)
754	Peach-lt. (Arms)
321	Christmas Red (Body)
799	Delft-med. (long straight edge of Hat)
798	Delft-dk. (angled edges of Hat, Body)
310	Black (Body)

Double Gold Metallic

DG2C Gold (Arms)

SANTA

Stitch on clear Plastic Canvas 10 over one bar.

Cut Size

Santa Hat (cut and stitch one)	9" x 5"
Santa Arm (cut and stitch two)	4" x 6"
Santa Body (cut and stitch one)	8" x 9"

STEP 1: Cross-stitch (one strand)

Skeins		DMC Floss	
1	—	White	
1	⊙	754	Peach-lt.
1	✗	760	Salmon
2		321	Christmas Red
1		798	Delft-dk.
1	●	310	Black

STEP 2: Half-cross (one strand)

Cards		Double Gold Metallic
1		DG2C Gold

STEP 3: Long stitch and short stitch (four strands). Make long and short stitches at random to fill area.

Skeins		Marlitt	
1		800	White

STEP 4: Long stitch (one strand)

Cards		Estaz	
2		EZ02	White

STEP 5: Backstitch (one strand)

Skeins		DMC Floss	

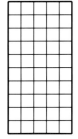

| 1 | 347 | Salmon-vy. dk. (mouth) |
| 1 | 435 | Brown-vy. lt. (eyes, nose) |

STEP 6: Trim and overcast (one strand). See Step 3 of Directions.

DMC Pearl Cotton #5

	White (long straight edge of hat; Body)
321	Christmas Red (angled edges of hat; Body)
798	Delft-dk. (Arms)
310	Black (Body)

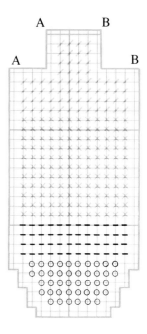

Soldier Arm
Stitch Count: 14 x 30

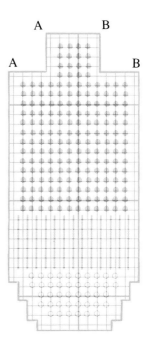

Santa Arm
Stitch Count: 14 x 31

Soldier Body
Stitch Count: 60 x 69

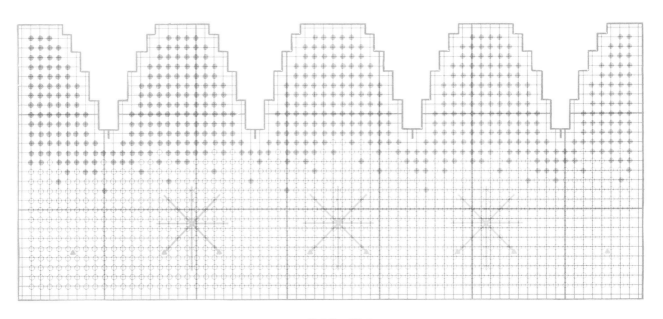

Soldier Hat
Stitch Count: 68 x 29

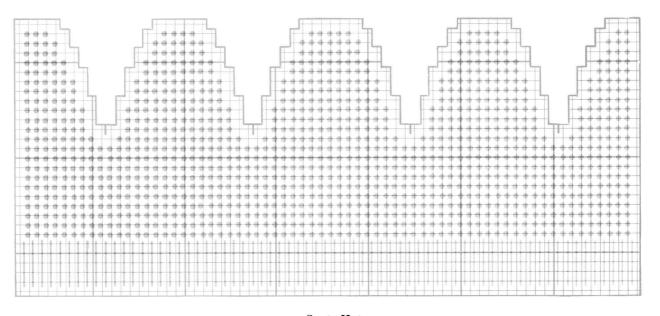

Santa Hat
Stitch Count: 68 x 29

Santa Body
Stitch Count: 60 x 69

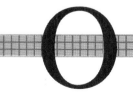O is for these ornaments so lovely and so rare,
They look as if Grandma very gently hung them there.
The flowers are the roses from the garden paths of old,
The colors are so brilliant with a tiny touch of gold.

Old World Charms

Finished sizes from left to right in the photos:
Ornament #1—4" W x 7" H x 4" D
Ornament #2—2¼" W x 9" H x 2¼" D
Ornament #3—2¼" W x 6½" H x 2½" D
Ornament #4—2¼" W x 6" H x 2¼" D

Materials for all ornaments

Materials for stitching (see Codes)
7 skeins of #327 DMC Pearl Cotton
  #5 for tassels
1 (½"-diameter) purple faceted glass bead
1 (½"-diameter) green faceted glass bead
5 (½"-diameter) pink faceted glass beads
Gold thread
1 (2" x 3") piece of cardboard

Directions

1. Stitch and trim plastic canvas pieces as directed in Codes.

2. To make Ornament #1, overcast long edges of Sides together. Whipstitch top edges together. Whipstitch bottom edges together. Center Bands vertically over each Side and whipstitch ends to top and bottom of Sides (see photo).

3. To make tassel, use one skein for each. Cut one 8" and one 5" piece of Pearl Cotton. Set aside. Wind remaining thread lengthwise over cardboard. Using the 5" piece of thread, weave through wrapped thread and tie a knot at top to secure. Cut threads at opposite end (Diagram 1).

Using 8" piece of thread, lay a narrow loop of yarn flat on tassel, looped end down and

extending below area to be wrapped (Diagram 2).

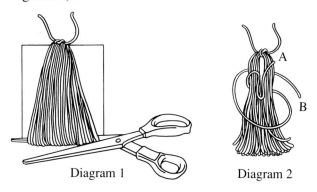

Diagram 1   Diagram 2

Wrap thread over the two strands that form the loop to secure. Then insert B through loop (Diagram 3). Pull up on A to secure loop and thread inside neck (Diagram 4).

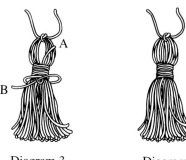

Diagram 3   Diagram 4

Cut off ends. Thread pink bead through tails of knot at top of tassel, then thread tails through bottom edge of ornament; secure (see photo).

4. For hanger, thread an 8" piece of gold thread through top of ornament. Make a loop; knot the ends.

5. To make Ornament #2, overcast one Top to widest short edge of each Side. Then overcast long edges of Sides together. Whipstitch bottom edges of Sides together.

Make tassel with purple bead (see Step 3 above). Attach to bottom of ornament. Make and attach hanger to top edge of ornament (see Step 4 above).

6. To make Ornament #3, overcast one Top to widest short edge of each Side. Then overcast long edges of Sides together. Whip-stitch bottom edges of Sides together.

Make and attach tassel/green bead at bottom edge of ornament (see Step 3 above). Make and attach hanger to bottom edge of ornament (see Step 4 above).

7. To make Ornament #4, overcast all edges of Sides together. Make four tassels with pink beads (see Step 3 above). Center and attach one tassel to the lowest point of the salmon stitching of each Side (see photo). Make and attach hanger (see Step 4 above).

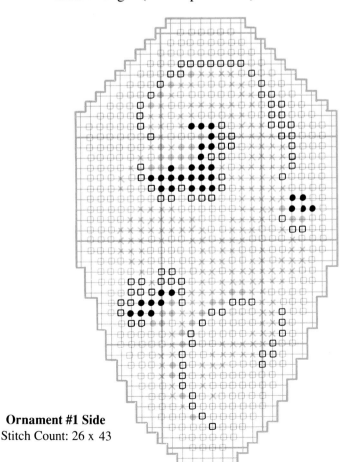

Ornament #1 Side
Stitch Count: 26 x 43

Codes

Stitch on clear Plastic Canvas 10 over one bar.

Cut Size

Ornament #1 (green bead):
Band (cut and stitch four)	3" x 8"
Side (cut and stitch four)	5" x 7"

Ornament #2 (purple bead):
Top (cut and stitch four)	4" x 4"
Side (cut and stitch four)	5" x 7"

Ornament #3 (pink bead):
Top (cut and stitch four)	4" x 4"
Side (cut and stitch four)	5" x 6"

Ornament #4 (cut and stitch four)	5" x 8"

STEP 1: Cross-stitch (six strands)

Skeins		DMC Floss	
4		676	Old Gold-lt. +
Spools	⊞	**Balger Cable**	
1		002P	Gold (one strand)

Skeins		DMC Floss	
1	✖	761	Salmon-lt.
2	●	760	Salmon
5	▫	347	Salmon-vy. dk.
2	●	327	Antique Violet-vy. dk.
3	✕	562	Jade-med.

STEP 2: Backstitch (two strands)

347   Salmon-vy. dk.

STEP 3: Trim and overcast (one strand)

Spools		**Balger ⅛"-wide Braided Ribbon**
1		002 Gold (see Directions)

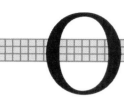

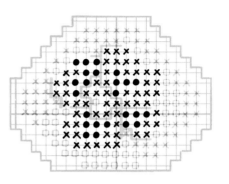

Ornament #2 Top
Stitch Count: 20 x 16

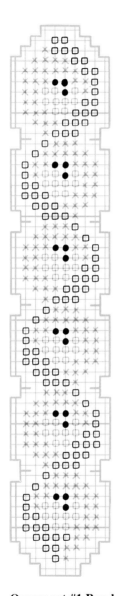

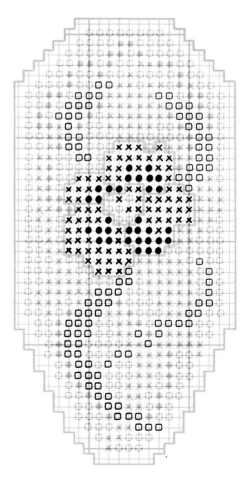

Ornament #1 Band
Stitch Count: 20 x 16

Ornament #2 Side
Stitch Count: 22 x 43

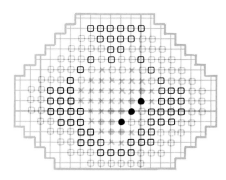

Ornament #3 Top
Stitch Count: 10 x 53

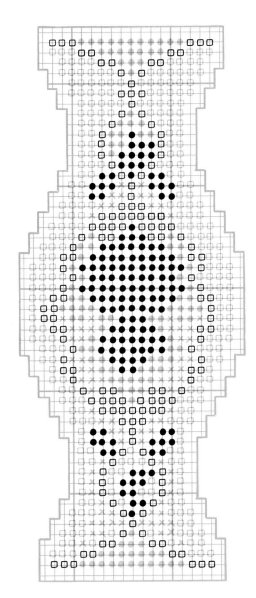

Ornament #4
Stitch Count: 23 x 54

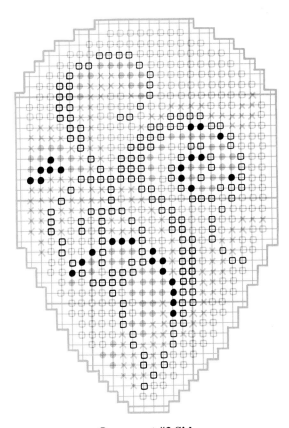

Ornament #3 Side
Stitch Count: 26 x 43

 is for the pictures, the ones you can't resist.
The ones you love the very most. Don't beg; we just insist,
That you take and carefully place them inside to send away,
To someone that is missed on this lovely springtime day.

═P icture This! ═

Finished sizes:

Small Frame—5¼" W x 5¼" H
Large Frame—4½" W x 10⅞" H

Materials for both frames

Materials for stitching (see Codes)
1 (10" x 12") piece of matte board
8" of ¼"-wide cream silk ribbon
   (see Suppliers)
Glue gun and glue
Craft knife

Directions

1. Stitch and trim plastic canvas pieces as directed in Codes.

2. Outline outer edges only of stitched Large Frame to make a pattern. Cut out pattern ⅛" from edges (Back). Using craft knife, cut one Back from matte board. Also from matte board, cut one 3" x 4½" piece (Stand). Mark a score line ¾" from one 3" edge of Stand. Fold along score line.

3. With bottom edges aligned, center and glue wrong side of top of Stand (above score line) to right side of Back. Cut ribbon in half. Place one end 1" from bottom edge of Back and centered horizontally; glue. Glue other end to wrong side of stand. (Remaining ribbon to be used on Small Frame.)

4. Center and glue Back to Large Frame, leaving one edge open. Allow to dry. Insert and center picture through open edge.

5. Repeat Steps 1-4 above to make the Small Frame.

Codes

LARGE FRAME

Stitch on clear Plastic Canvas 10 over one bar. The plastic canvas is cut 7" x 13". Cut and stitch one.

STEP 1: Padded long stitch (one strand)

Cards		Neon Rays	
2		N16	Pale Peach
2		N03	Pale Beige
2		N42	Taupe

STEP 2: Bosnia stitch (one strand)

	NO3	Pale Beige

STEP 3: Jessica stitch (one strand)

1	N29	Rust

STEP 4: Cross-stitch (four strands)

Skeins		Marlitt	
1		1019	Salmon-lt.

STEP 5: Trim and overcast (one strand)

	Neon Rays	
	N16	Pale Peach (around openings)
	N42	Taupe (all else)

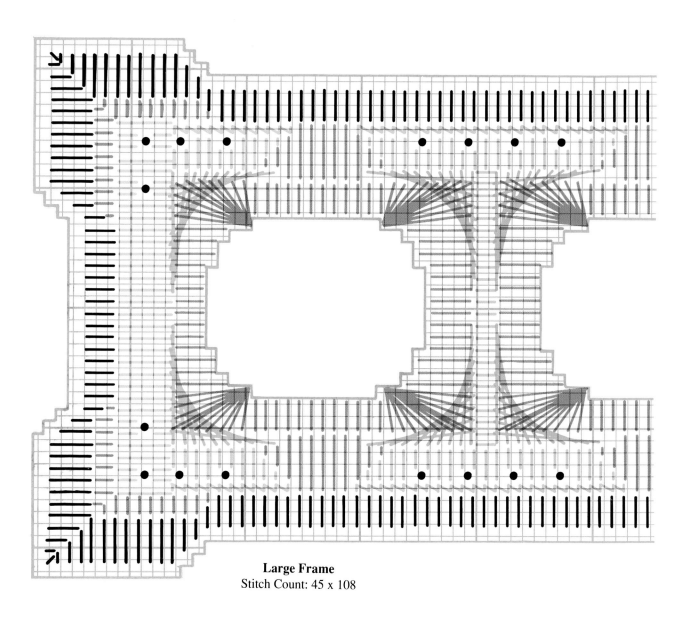

Large Frame
Stitch Count: 45 x 108

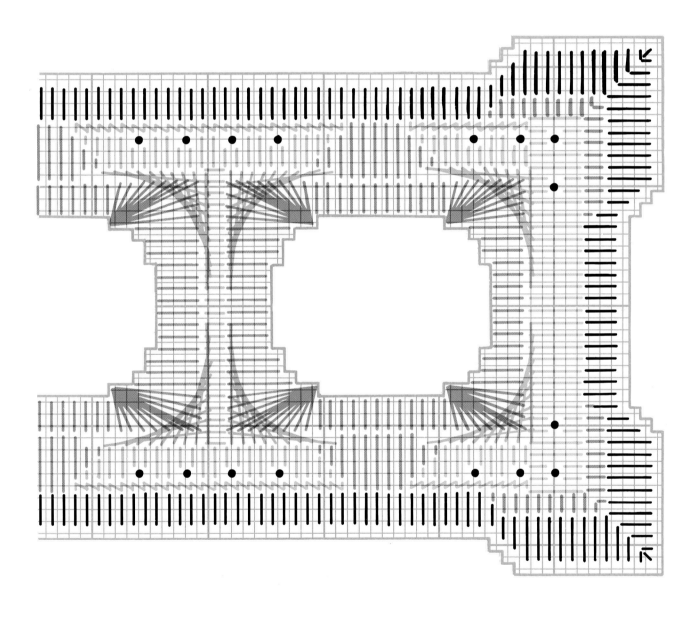

SMALL FRAME

Stitch on clear Plastic Canvas 10 over one bar. The plastic canvas is cut 8" x 8". Cut and stitch one.

STEP 1: Padded long stitch (one strand)

Cards		Neon Rays	
1		N16	Pale Peach
2		N03	Pale Beige
2		N42	Taupe

STEP 2: Bosnia stitch (one strand)

Skeins		Sew Your Wild Threads	
1		107	Chill
Cards		Neon Rays	
		N03	Pale Beige

STEP 3: Jessica stitch (one strand)

1		N29	Rust

STEP 4: Trim and overcast (one strand)

	N42	Taupe (all cut edges)

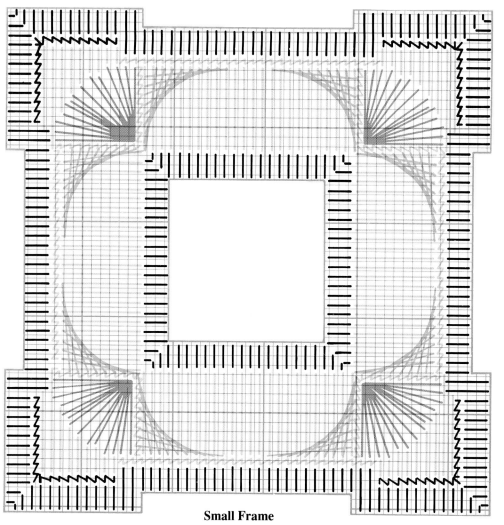

Small Frame
Stitch Count: 53 x 53

Q is for the quiet now to hear the snowflake fall.
It is my favorite miracle that I can ere recall.
I love to sit beside the fire with needlework in hand,
and remake whatever Nature does—oh, isn't she just grand!

Queen Anne's Lace

Finished sizes:

Snowflakes A, B and C—4½" W x 4½" H

SNOWFLAKE A

Stitch on clear Plastic Canvas 10 over one bar. The plastic canvas is cut 6" x 6". Cut and stitch two.

STEP 1: Trim and overcast (one strand)

Cards		Estaz
2		EZ02 White (all outer edges)

STEP 2: Long stitch (one strand)

Skeins		Sew Your Wild Threads
1		218 Emotion
Spools		**Balger Blending Filament**
1		001 Silver

STEP 3: Center design (one strand). Place snowflakes together with wrong sides facing, centers matching and points alternating between each other. Stitch through both layers. Thread beads on Balger and weave vertically through center of one snowflake, diagonally through the other; see graph.

		001 Silver
Beads		**Mill Hill Beads**
18		00161 Crystal

STEP 4: Overcast (three strands)

Skeins		DMC Floss
1		White (inside circle)

STEP 5: Make loop (three 6" strands). Thread through center between two points of snowflake; knot ends to make a loop.

		Balger Blending Filament
		001 Silver

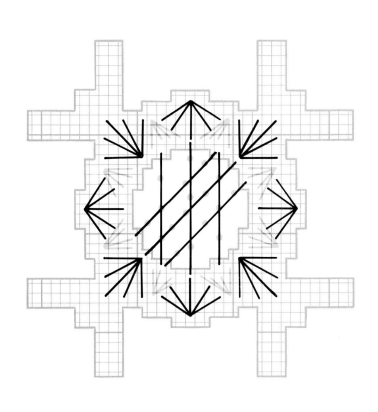

Snowflake A
Stitch Count: 34 x 34

SNOWFLAKE B

Stitch on clear Plastic Canvas 10 over one bar. The plastic canvas is cut 6" x 6". Cut and stitch two.

STEP 1: Long stitch (one strand)

Skeins		Sew Your Wild Threads
1		1308 Glitz

STEP 2: Rhodes stitch (one strand)

Cards		Cresta d' Oro
1		C15 Snow

STEP 3: Jessica stitch (one strand)

		Patina
1		PA30 Ice Blue

STEP 4: Trim and overcast (one strand). Overcast outer edges of each snowflake. Place snowflakes together with right sides up, centers matching and points alternating between each other.

	Cresta d' Oro
	C15 Snow

STEP 5: Make loop (two strands). Thread through center between two points of snowflake; knot ends to make a loop.

	Sew Your Wild Threads
	1308 Glitz

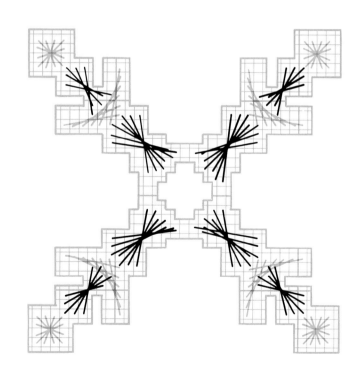

Snowflake B
Stitch Count: 34 x 34

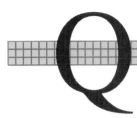

SNOWFLAKE C

Stitch on clear Plastic Canvas 10 over one bar. The plastic was cut 6" x 6". Cut and stitch two.

STEP 1: Long stitch (one strand)

Skeins		Sew Your Wild Threads
1		105 Chill
Cards		**Cresta d' Oro**
1		C15 Snow

STEP 2: Rhodes stitch (one strand). Stitch center of one snowflake only.

		Sew Your Wild Threads
		105 Chill
Spools		**Balger Blending Filament**
1		014 Sky Blue

STEP 3: Backstitch (one strand)

	Sew Your Wild Threads
	105 Chill

STEP 4: Trim and overcast (one strand). Overcast outer edges of each snowflake. Place snowflakes with right sides up, centers matching, and points alternating between each other.

	105 Chill

STEP 5: Make loop (two strands). Thread through center between two points of snowflake; knot ends to make a loop.

	Balger Blending Filament
	014 Sky Blue

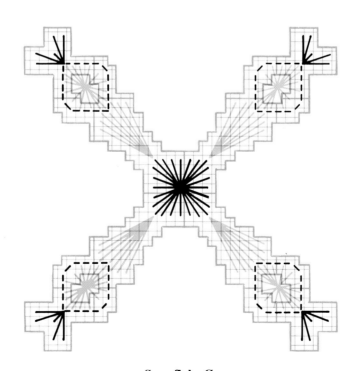

Snowflake C
Stitch Count: 34 x 34

R is for the rings that do need a special place
As lovely and as royal as this tiny little case.
Somewhere new to hide them when never worn around,
Now you'll know right where they are when you need them to be found.

Royal Ring Boxes

BLUE RING BOX

Finished size: 3¾" W x 3¾" H x 2" D

Materials

Materials for stitching (see Codes)

2 (15 bars x 20 bars) pieces of unstitched clear Plastic Canvas 10 (Liner As)

4 (13 bars x 20 bars) pieces of unstitched clear Plastic Canvas 10 (Liner Bs)

Directions

1. Stitch and trim plastic canvas pieces as directed in Codes.

2. To make box, overcast long edges of three Sides together in the following order: A, B, A. Repeat with remaining Side As and Side B. Overcast A/B/A sections together on side edges. Overcast Bottom to Sides, with stitching facing out. Overcast top edge of Sides.

3. To make liner, repeat Step 2 above with unstitched plastic Liner As and Liner Bs. Insert inside box.

4. To make lid, overcast one long edge of Rim A to short edges of Lid A. Repeat with remaining Lids and matching Rims. Then overcast long edges of three Rims/Lids together in the following order: A, B, A. Repeat with remaining As and B. Overcast A/B/A sections together on side edges. Overcast bottom edges of Rims. Place the lid on box.

Codes

Stitch on clear Plastic Canvas 10 over one bar.

	Cut Size
Side A (cut and stitch 4)	4" x 4"
Side B (cut and stitch 2)	4" x 4"
Lid A (cut and stitch 4)	4" x 4"
Lid B (cut and stitch 2)	4" x 4"
Rim A (cut and stitch 4)	4" x 3"
Rim B (cut and stitch 2)	4" x 3"
Bottom (cut and stitch 2)	6" x 4"

STEP 1: Scotch stitch (one strand)

Skeins

5

Watercolours

Tropic Seas

STEP 2: Continental stitch and reverse continental stitch (one strand)

Tropic Seas

STEP 3: Smyrna cross-stitch (one strand)

Tropic Seas

STEP 4: Long stitch (one strand)

Tropic Seas

STEP 5: Short stitch (one strand)

Tropic Seas

STEP 6: Trim and overcast (one strand)

Tropic Seas (see Steps 2-4 of Directions)

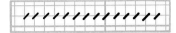

Rim A
Stitch Count: 14 x 3

Rim B
Stitch Count: 16 x 3

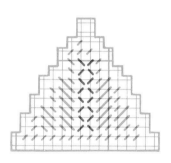

Lid A
Stitch Count: 16 x 14

Side A
Stitch Count: 14 x 17

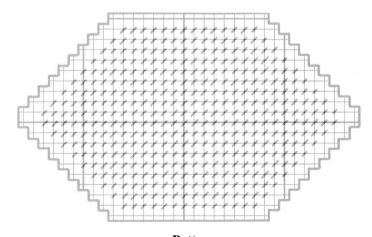

Bottom
Stitch Count: 34 x 20

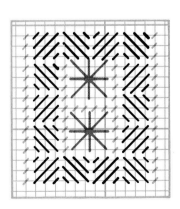

Side B
Lid B
Stitch Count: 16 x 17

LAVENDER RING BOX

Finished Size: 3¼" W x 3½" H x 3¼" D

Materials

Materials for stitching (see Codes)
1 (6" x 6") piece of unstitched Plastic
Canvas 10

Directions:

1. Stitch and trim plastic canvas pieces as directed in Codes.

2. To make box, overcast inner edge of Rim. Overcast short edges of Sides together to form an open box. Then overcast Bottom to one edge with stitching facing out. Overcast Rim to remaining edge with the stitching facing out.

3. To make lid, outline outer edge only of stitched Layer D to make a pattern for Lid Bottom. Trim one bar from all edges. Set aside.

Overcast all long edges of Handle. Whip-stitch short edges of Handle to center of Handle/Layer A (see photo). Then overcast edges of Layer A to unstitched area on top of Layer B. Repeat process for Layers C and D. Place unstitched Lid Bottom under Layer D and overcast. Place lid on box.

Codes

Stitch on clear Plastic Canvas 10 over one bar.

	Cut Size
Rim (cut and stitch one)	6" x 6"
Side (cut and stitch four)	5" x 4"
Handle (cut and stitch one)	4" x 4"
Layer A (cut and stitch one)	4" x 4"
Layer B (cut and stitch one)	5" x 5"
Layer C (cut and stitch one)	5" x 5"
Layer D (cut and stitch one)	6" x 6"
Bottom (cut and stitch one)	6" x 6"

STEP 1: Continental stitch (one strand)

Skeins		Watercolours
5		Lavender Mist

STEP 2: Long stitch (one strand)

Lavender Mist

Lavender Mist

STEP 3: Trim and overcast (one strand)

Lavender Mist (see Steps 2 and 3 of Directions)

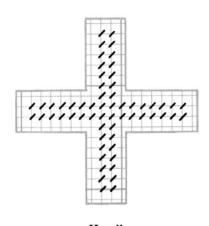

Handle
Stitch Count: 18 x 18

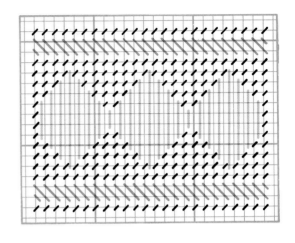

Side
Stitch Count: 26 x 20

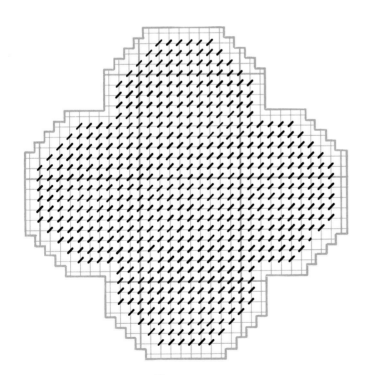

Bottom
Stitch Count: 32 x 32

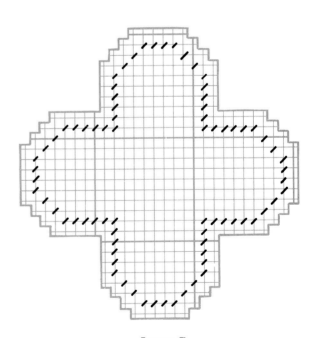

Layer C
Stitch Count: 28 x 28

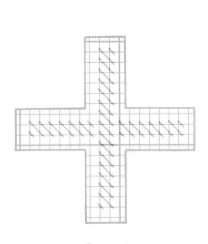

Layer A
Stitch Count: 18 x 18

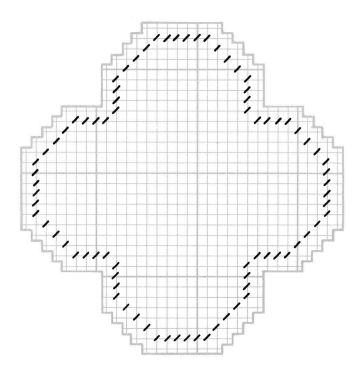

Layer D
Stitch Count: 32 x 32

Rim
Stitch Count: 32 x 32

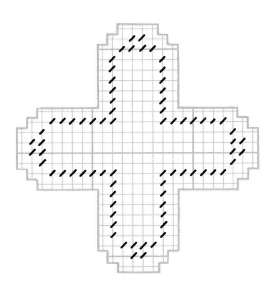

Layer B
Stitch Count: 24 x 24

S is for a star-shaped box in which you put your hat,
A reminder of time gone by when I first realized that
Stars are magic, so they say; I know that they are right,
For they shoot through darkened skies on a warm midsummer's night.

Starry Sensation

HAT BOX

Finished size: 15" W x 10½" H x 15" D

Materials:

Materials for stitching (see Codes)
1 (3' x 3') piece of unstitched clear Plastic
    Canvas 10
¾ yard of peach moiré taffeta (optional, see
    Step 7)
3½ yards of ½"-wide peach braid
1 (15" x 15") piece of corrugated cardboard
1 (10" x 10" x 8") corrugated cardboard box
1 (3"-long) purchased peach tassel
1 package of T pins
Tacky Glue (see Suppliers)

Directions

1. Stitch and trim plastic canvas pieces as directed in Codes.

2. Using the stitched pieces as patterns, cut the following from unstitched plastic canvas: four of Side B, Rims A, B and C, and Lids A, B and C; one Bottom (see pattern on pg. 108).

The hat box is constructed by handling the stitched pieces and the following unstitched plastic canvas pieces as one.

3. To make top of lid, overcast the following together on the long edges: one Lid A to one Lid B, then left edge of one Lid C to right edge of A/B section. Repeat to make four Lid A/B/C sections. Overcast these together on the long edges to make top of lid (the pieces will not lie flat, see photo).

4. To make rim of lid, overcast one Rim A and one Rim B together on the 2½" edges. Then overcast left 1½" edge of one Rim C to right 1½" edge of A/B section. Repeat to make four Rim A/B/C sections. Overcast these together on the short edges to make rim. Overcast top to rim to make lid, matching peaks of Rim A/Bs with Lid A/Bs.

5. To make box, overcast the following together on the long edges: one Side A to another Side A, then left edge of one Side B to right edge of A/A section. Repeat to make four Side A/A/B sections. Overcast the long edges of these together to form an open box. Overcast the bottom edge of box (edge with more stitched flowers, see photo) to unstitched Bottom. Overcast remaining edges of box.

6. To embellish lid, cut four 18" pieces from the peach braid and glue each on the seam between the Lid and Rim A/B/C sections. Center and attach tassel to top of lid. Then glue remaining piece of braid on the seam between the top and rim, overlapping ends.

7. Insert cardboard box inside plastic canvas box. Stabilize the curves by securing a T pin through the plastic canvas walls into the cardboard on each side of the curve.

Optional: For a more finished look, the cardboard box can be lined and covered with taffeta. Also, to line lid, cut one Bottom from cardboard, omitting ⅛" on all edges. Cover with taffeta. Insert in lid.

Codes

Stitch on clear Plastic Canvas 10 over one bar.

	Cut Size
Lid A (cut and stitch four)	5" x 10"
Lid B (cut and stitch four)	5" x 10"
Lid C (cut and stitch four)	8" x 9"
Rim A (cut and stitch four)	5" x 5"
Rim B (cut and stitch four)	5" x 5"
Rim C (cut and stitch four)	9" x 4"
Side A (cut and stitch eight)	5" x 11"
Side B (cut and stitch four)	9" x 11"

STEP 1: Cross-stitch (six strands)

Skeins		DMC Floss	
3	⊙	677	Old Gold-vy. lt.
90	—	3774	Peach Pecan-med.
4	△	761	Salmon-lt.
3	▲	760	Salmon
11	⊡	3727	Antique Mauve-lt.
8	▣	316	Antique Mauve-med.
3	▲	961	Wild Rose-dk.
2	✳	519	Sky Blue
6	✕	368	Pistachio Green-lt.
9	⊕	503	Blue Green-med.
14	●	502	Blue Green

STEP 2: Trim and overcast (twelve strands)

	3774	Peach Pecan-med. (see Directions)

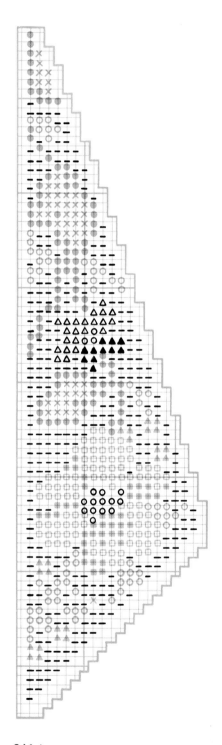

Lid A
Stitch Count: 21 x 73

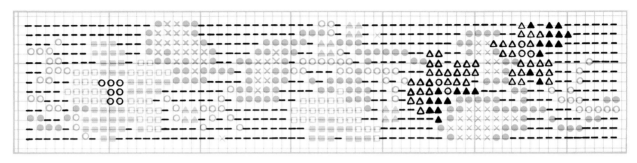

Rim C
Stitch Count: 67 x 15

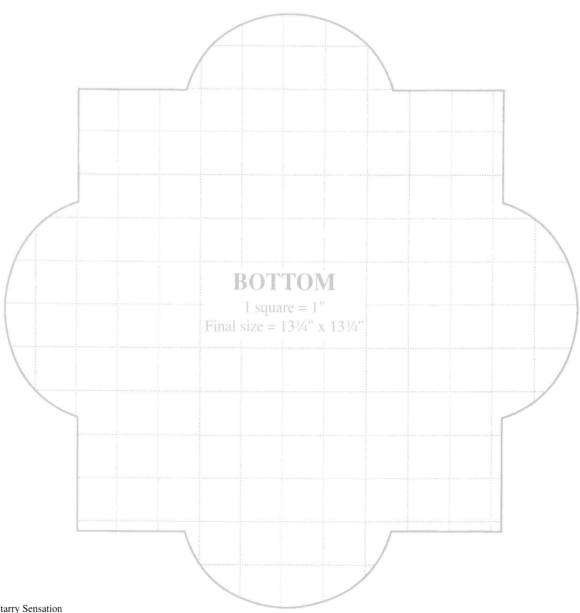

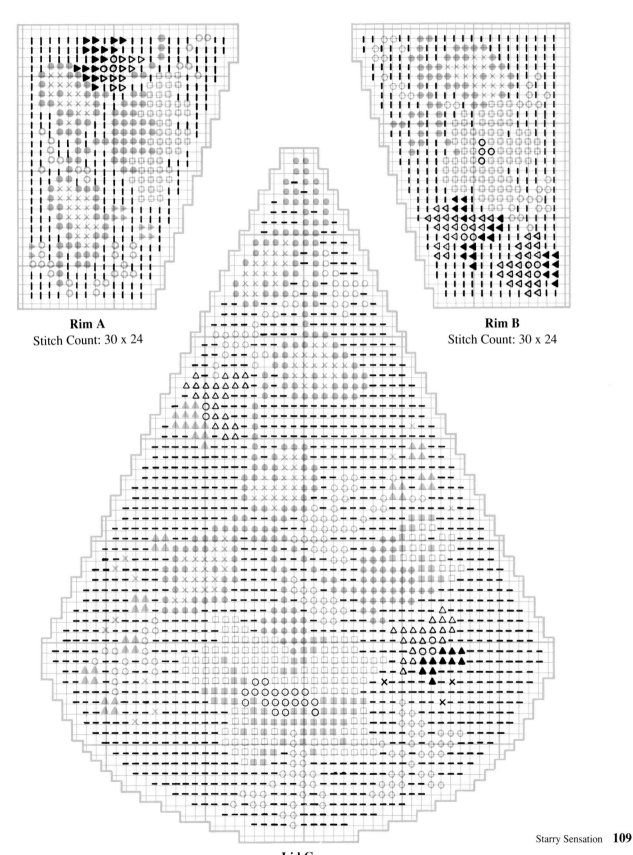

Rim A
Stitch Count: 30 x 24

Rim B
Stitch Count: 30 x 24

Lid C
Stitch Count: 52 x 68

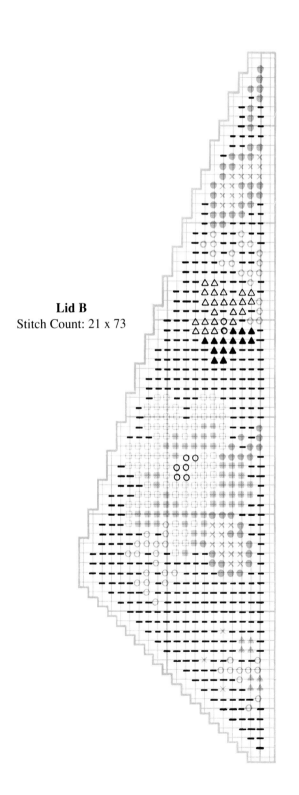

Lid B
Stitch Count: 21 x 73

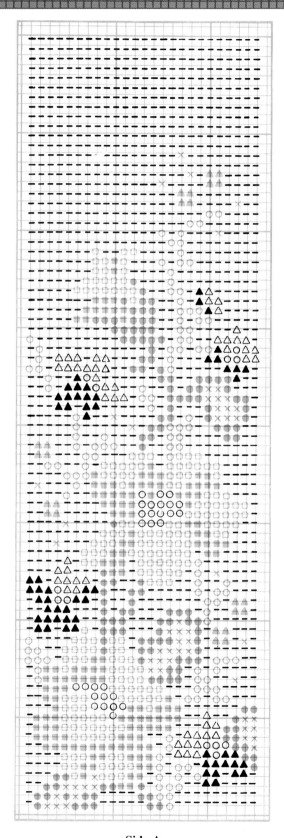

Side A
Stitch Count: 27 x 82

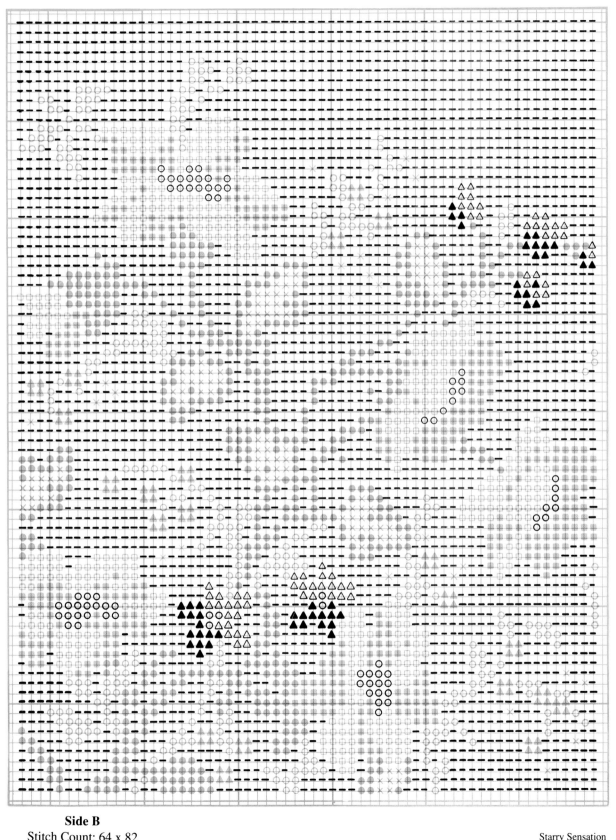

Side B
Stitch Count: 64 x 82

T is for this toy shelf and the tissue box, it's true.
They're for the very young and old. Excuse me, please, achoo!
A night stand is a splendid place for either one of these,
So hand to me a hanky, and hurry, if you please.

Tried and True

TISSUE BOX

Finished size: 4¾" W x 5½" H x 4¾" D

Stitch on clear Plastic Canvas 10 over one bar. The plastic canvas was cut 7" x 7". Cut and stitch four Sides and one Top.

STEP 1: Cross-stitch (one strand)

Skeins		DMC Pearl Cotton #5	
1	✖		Ecru
1	—	819	Baby Pink-lt.
1	⊡	224	Shell Pink-lt.
1	○	800	Delft-pale

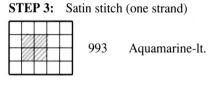

1		598	Turquoise-lt.
1		966	Baby Green-med.

STEP 2: Padded satin stitch (one strand)

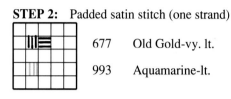

1	677	Old Gold-vy. lt.
1	993	Aquamarine-lt.

STEP 3: Satin stitch (one strand)

	993	Aquamarine-lt.

Codes continued on next page

Top
Stitch Count: 46 x 46

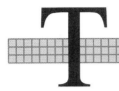

STEP 4:   Backstitch (one strand)

Skeins		DMC Floss	
1		924	Slate Green-vy. dk.

STEP 5:   Continental stitch (one strand)

DMC Pearl Cotton #5

   Ecru (Top)

800   Delft-pale (Sides)

STEP 6:   Trim and overcast (one strand)

Ecru (all edges of Top)

800   Delft-pale (all edges of Sides)

STEP 7:   Whipstitch (one strand). Whipstitch Sides together on long edges. Then whipstitch Top to Sides.

966   Baby Green-med.

Side
Stitch Count: 46 x 55

Tiny Tots Toyshelf

Finished size: 5" W x 7½" H x 2¾" D

Materials

Materials for stitching (see Codes)
Music box movement #570 (see
    Suppliers)
Assorted miniature toys for shelves*
1 (½"-long) gold bugle beads*
Glue gun and glue
Curved needle
*available from craft store

Directions

1. Stitch and trim plastic canvas pieces as directed in Codes.

2. Using #90591 Windrush Yarn, overcast Top/Front to Back/Sides on all corners.

Using #90100 Windrush Yarn, overcast inner edges of Front, catching outer edges of each Shelf in stitches. Overcast decorative top edges of Front and Sides (see photo).

3. Glue music box movement to wrong side of Back, placing stem through hole.

4. Using #90591 Windrush Yarn and the curved needle, overcast Base to bottom edge of shelf where indicated by graph.

5. Glue miniature toys to shelves where desired. Sew bugle beads to front of Drawer B at each ● (see graph). Screw key to music box movement stem.

Codes

Stitch on clear Plastic Canvas 7 over one bar.

	Cut Size
Front (cut and stitch one)	7" x 9"
Back (cut and stitch one)	7" x 9"
Side (cut and stitch two)	5" x 9"
Base (cut and stitch one)	7" x 5"
Shelf (cut and stitch two)	7" x 5"
Top (cut and stitch one)	7" x 5"
Drawer A (cut and stitch one)	6" x 4"
Drawer B (cut and stitch one)	6" x 3"

STEP 1: Continental and reverse continental stitch (one strand). Stitch each Shelf and Top. Then, stitch Back, beginning at the bottom. When you have stitched to "Shelf Placement" on the graph, position long edge of one Shelf perpendicular to Back. Continue stitching, catching edge of Shelf with each stitch. Repeat to attach second Shelf to Back. Then stitch Sides, catching remaining side edges of same Shelves in stitching. For Front, repeat process to catch Top in stitching.

Skein		Windrush Yarn
1		90100 Ecru
1		90591 Jade

STEP 2:   Trim and overcast (one strand)

90100 Ecru (all edges of
Drawer A; outer edges of Base;
Front and Sides, see Step 2 of
Directions)

90591 Jade (see Steps
2 and 4 of Directions)

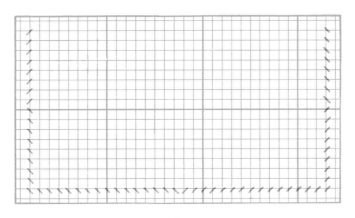

Base
Stitch Count: 34 x 19

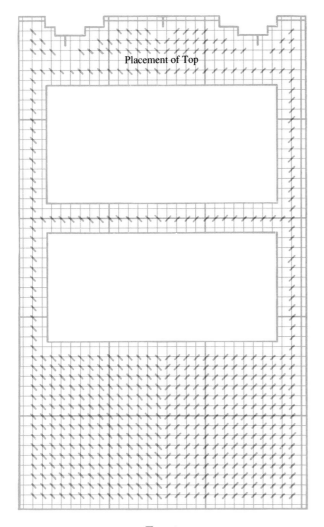

Placement of Top

Front
Stitch Count: 26 x 12

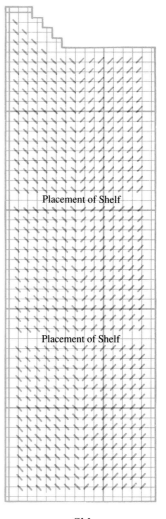

Placement of Shelf

Placement of Shelf

Side
Stitch Count: 16 x 50

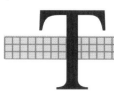

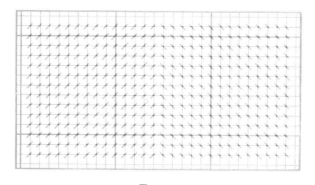

**Top
Shelf**
Stitch Count: 30 x 16

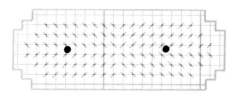

Drawer B
Stitch Count: 22 x 8

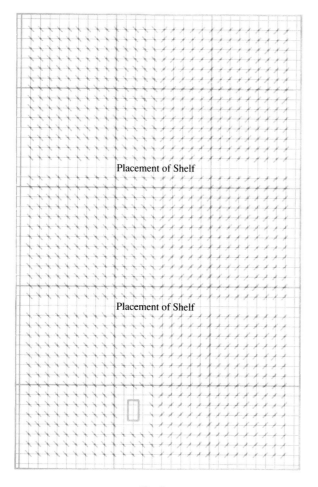

Placement of Shelf

Placement of Shelf

Back
Stitch Count: 30 x 46

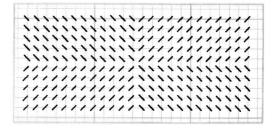

Drawer A
Stitch Count: 26 x 12

U is for undying love, and always it takes two,
Like little furry bunnies who love to kiss—I know they do!
They sit upon a block that matches any type of room,
And play their music through the day, but not before the noon.

⊞■ Undying Love ▦▦▦

BUNNY MUSIC BOX

Finished size: 4¼" W x 9" H x 4¼" D

Materials

Materials for stitching (see Codes)
1 (30 x 30 bars) piece of unstitched
    Plastic Canvas 7
1 (22" x 22") piece of ⅛"-thick Masonite
1 music box movement #571*
2 (6"-high) stuffed bunnies*
¼ yard each of ¼"-wide pink and blue
    satin ribbon
½ yard of ⅛"-wide mauve silk ribbon*
1 (1¾"-wide) wood bowl**
5 dried rosettes**
7 (1½"-long) plastic carrots**
Acrylic paints
Drill and ¼" bit
Glue gun and glue
*see Suppliers
**available at craft store

Directions

1. Stitch and trim plastic canvas pieces as directed in Codes.

2. Cut four 3⅞" x 3⅞" pieces (Sides) and one 3¾" x 3¾" piece (Top) from Masonite. Drill a ½"-diameter hole in the center of one Side. Center and mark ½" from one edge of Top. Drill a ½"-wide hole at mark. Set aside all Masonite pieces.

3. Remove key and waggie from music box movement. On back of Side with hole, insert stem in hole and glue. Glue Sides together to form an open box. Attach waggie to music movement. Glue Top to Sides with the waggie through the hole (Diagram 1).

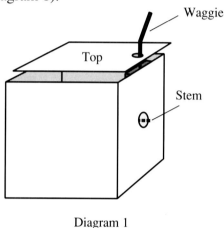

Diagram 1

4. To make plastic canvas box, overcast holes in stitched Top and Side with hole. Overcast Sides together to form an open box. Overcast Top to Sides, placing waggie through hole. Glue Masonite box inside plastic canvas box with holes and open edges matching. Overcast unstitched plastic canvas piece to bottom.

5. For female bunny, tie pink ribbon in a bow around neck. For male bunny, make a bow tie from blue ribbon. Glue female bunny near one corner of box (see photo). With scissors, make a hole in bottom of right foot on male bunny. Insert music movement waggie in hole.

6. Paint wood bowl as desired. Glue four carrots and three rosettes in bowl. Glue bowl in front of bunnies. Glue remaining rosettes near bottom side of bowl (see photo). Cut mauve ribbon in half. Tie pieces together in a bow around greens of remaining plastic carrots. Glue carrot bunch in paw of one bunny.

Codes

Stitch on clear Plastic Canvas 7 over one bar.

Side: Cut and stitch four 6" x 6" pieces. Stitch three pieces following graph. On fourth piece, cut one ½"-diameter hole in center. Stitch following graph.

Top: Cut and stitch one 30 bar x 30 bar piece. See STEP 3 below.

STEP 1: Cross-stitch (one strand)

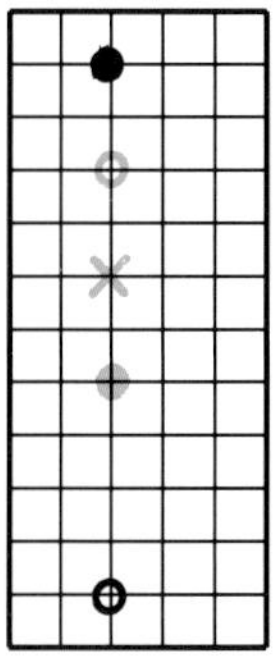

Skeins		**Pearl Cotton DMC #3**	
1	●	223	Shell Pink-med.
1	◉	519	Sky Blue
1	✕	518	Wedgewood-lt.
1	✦	806	Peacock Blue-dk.
Cards		**Overture** (two strands)	
14	⊙	V52	Normandy

STEP 2: Backstitch (one strand)

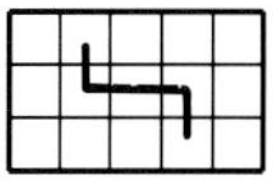

Pearl Cotton DMC #3

806   Peacock Blue-dk.

STEP 3: Cross-stitch Top (two strands). Mark ½" from one edge of unstitched plastic canvas, centered horizontally. Cut a ½"-wide hole at mark. Cross-stitch 28 x 28 stitches There is no graph for this piece.

Overture

V52   Normandy

STEP 4: Trim and overcast (four strands)

V52   Normandy (see Step 4 of Directions)

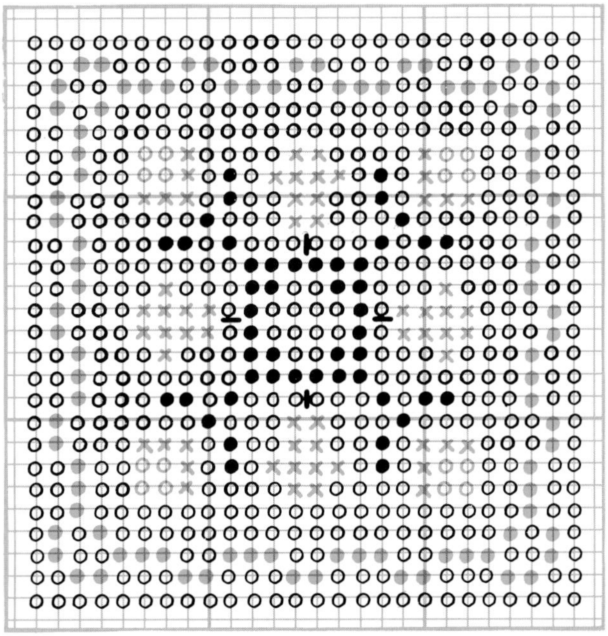

Side
Stitch Count: 28 x 28

V is for small violets and valentines and hearts,
That are delivered just for you in this tiny little cart,
I made them all myself and it's easy just to see.
They are for someone that I love. Whoever could that be?

■ Very Truly Yours ▦▦▦

Finished size: 7½" W x 5½" H x 4" D

Materials

Materials for stitching (see Codes)
¼ yard of light pink satin
1¾ yards of ⅛"-wide light pink silk ribbon*
2¼ yards of ⅛"-wide pink silk ribbon*
¼ yard of ⅛"-wide rose silk ribbon*
½ yard of ⅛"-wide dark red silk ribbon*
30 (2-mm) light pink iridescent pearl beads
Stuffing
Glue gun and glue
*see Suppliers

Directions

1. Stitch and trim plastic canvas pieces as directed in Codes.

2. Cut Medium Hearts and Small Hearts from satin according to patterns (pg. 125). Stitch two Medium Hearts together with right sides facing, leaving an opening. Clip cleavage. Turn. Stuff firmly. Slipstitch opening closed. Repeat to make seven Medium Hearts and eight Small Hearts.

3. Construct cart following Steps 2 and 3 of *Country Cart* (pg. 22).

4. Make 19 small pink carnations using pink silk ribbon. Glue one carnation to every other point at top of cart. Glue one bead to remaining points.

Glue four small carnations to make a round bouquet in center of each wheel. Glue one bead in center of bouquet. Glue eight beads evenly spaced on outer edge of bouquet (see photo).

5. Cut light pink ribbon in four equal pieces. Handling as one, tie ribbons in a bow. Glue to side of cart in back (see photo). Cut remaining ribbons in various lengths. Thread one ribbon through cleavage of one stitched Small Heart, making tails of even lengths. Repeat for remaining Small Hearts. Gather tails together and secure through top edge of cart, letting them dangle from light pink ribbons (see photo).

6. Stuff cart to within 1" of top edge. Arrange satin hearts and remaining stitched Hearts on stuffing; glue as needed to keep all of the hearts stationary.

Codes

Stitch on clear Plastic Canvas 10 over one bar. The graphs for the Wheel, End and Side are on pg. 24.

Cut Size

Stand (cut and stitch two) 4" x 5"
Wheel (cut and stitch four) 6" x 6"
Handle A (cut and stitch two) 6" x 3"
Handle B (cut and stitch two) 6" x 3"
Bottom (cut and stitch one) 7" x 6"
End (cut and stitch two) 6" x 5"
Side (cut and stitch two) 8" x 5"

Stitch on clear Plastic Canvas 7 over one bar.

Heart A (cut and stitch four) 3" x 3"
Heart B (cut and stitch seven) 4" x 4"
Heart C (cut and stitch seven) 5" x 4"

STEP 1: Continental stitch (one strand)

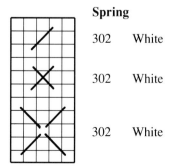

Skeins		Spring	
3		302	White
		302	White (Wheels)
Skeins		**DMC Pearl Cotton #3**	
1		3689	Mauve-lt. (two strands)
1		899	Rose-med. (two strands)
1		309	Rose-dp. (two strands)

STEP 2: Long stitch (one strand)

Spring

302 White

302 White

302 White

STEP 3: Upright cross-stitch (one strand)

302 White

STEP 4: Cross-stitch (one strand)

302 White

STEP 5: Cross-stitch Bottom (one strand). Stitch 45 x 29 stitches. There is no graph for this piece.

302 White

STEP 6: Backstitch (one strand)

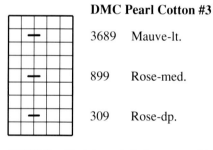

DMC Pearl Cotton #3

3689 Mauve-lt.

899 Rose-med.

309 Rose-dp.

STEP 7: Parisian stitch (two strands)

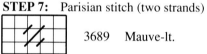

3689 Mauve-lt.

STEP 8: Trim and overcast (one strand)

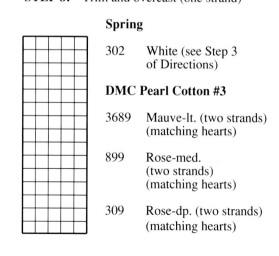

Spring

302 White (see Step 3 of Directions)

DMC Pearl Cotton #3

3689 Mauve-lt. (two strands) (matching hearts)

899 Rose-med. (two strands) (matching hearts)

309 Rose-dp. (two strands) (matching hearts)

Handle A
Stitch Count: 33 x 9

Heart A
Stitch Count: 6 x 5

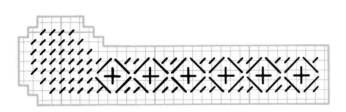

Handle B
Stitch Count: 33 x 9

Heart C
Stitch Count: 15 x 12

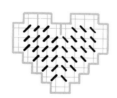

Heart B
Stitch Count: 10 x 8

MEDIUM HEART
Cut 14
Add ¼" seam allowances to all edges.

SMALL HEART
Cut 16
Add ¼" seam allowances to all edges.

W is for a wonderland covered with winter's snow,
It's a very cheery music box to play by the fire's glow.
The tiny drummer squirrel bangs out a Christmas tune,
As three jolly Santa's helpers march around the room.

Winter Wonderland

Finished size: 8" W x 7½" H x 8" D

Materials

Materials for stitching (see Codes)
1 (6") circle of unstitched plastic
  canvas (Top)*
1 (17¼" x 1⅝") piece of unstitched plastic
  canvas (Side)*
¼ yard of 45"-wide blue print fabric
1 music box movement #572*
Craft miniatures to create winter scene
  (see photo)**
Ceramic beads for embellishments
  (see photo)**
Stuffing
Glue gun and glue
*see Suppliers
**available at craft stores

Directions

1. Stitch and trim plastic canvas pieces as directed in Codes.

2. Overcast short edges of unstitched Side together, then overcast one long edge to stitched Bottom to make a round box. Glue music box movement inside Bottom, placing stem through center hole. Stuff box firmly. Overcast unstitched Top to top of box.

3. To make shirring, cut one 2¾" x 45" strip from fabric. Fold both long edges ¼" to the wrong side. Sew gathering threads through both layers on long edges. Shirr (gather) strip to fit around box. Overlap and slipstitch ends of shirring together. Align folded long edge of shirring with top edge of box;

whipstitch. Pull lower edge of shirring under box. Gather snugly. Whipstitch to Bottom.

4. To make binding, cut one 1" x 22" bias strip from fabric. Fold long edges ¼" to wrong side; press. Slipstitch one folded edge of ¼" from edge on top of Star, forming a corner at each point (see photo). Slipstitch remaining edge to wrong side of Star. Center and glue Star on box.

5. Embellish music box with craft miniatures and ceramic beads (see photo). Screw base to music box movement stem.

Codes

Star: Stitch on clear Plastic Canvas 7 over one bar. The plastic canvas is cut 9" x 9". Cut and stitch one.

Bottom: Stitch on clear Plastic Canvas 6" circle (see Suppliers). Cut and stitch one (see STEP 4 below).

STEP 1: Cross-stitch (one strand)

Skeins		DMC Pearl Cotton #3
1	●	White

STEP 2: Upright cross stitch (three strands)

Cards		Overture	
1	┼	V40	Tidal Pool

STEP 3: Couched thread (three strands)

		V40	Tidal Pool
			couched with
		V40	Tidal Pool

Codes continued on next page.

STEP 4: Long stitch Bottom (three strands). Beginning one bar from outside edge of circle, stitch toward center over eight bars. Repeat around entire circle. Cut out center circle, beginning one bar from stitched area.

V40   Tidal Pool

STEP 5: Trim and overcast (three strands)

V40   Tidal Pool (all)

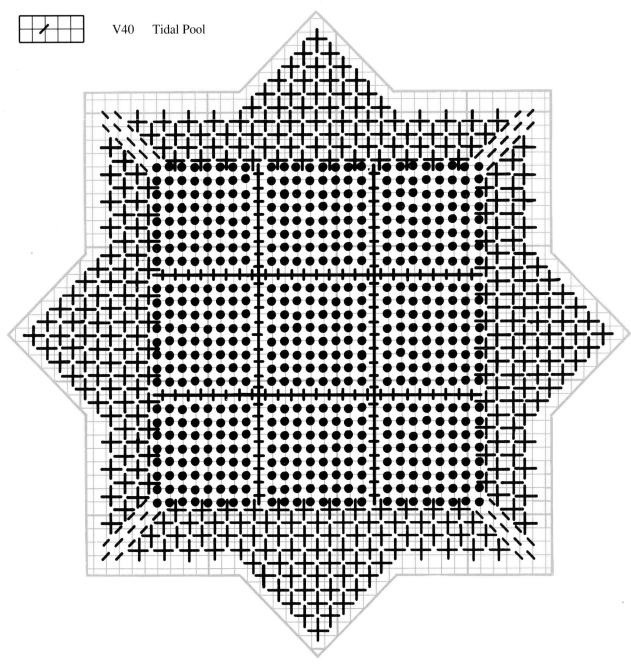

Star
Stitch Count: 48 x 48

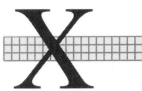

X is for "x"pressly a cake for two,
I heard that it's your wedding and I know that it is true,
You are the special loved ones who have come upon this day,
To join your hands together whatever comes your way.

"X"pressly Yours

Finished size: 7¼" W x 11" x 7¼" D

Directions

1. Stitch and trim plastic canvas pieces as
directed in Codes.

2. To make base, overcast short edges of Base
Band together. Overcast Base Bottom to one
edge of Base Band to form a round box.
Stuff firmly. Overcast Base Top to Base
Band.

3. Overcast Trellises together on short straight
edges so that they form a right angle. Then
overcast one Archway to each end of Trellis
(see photo). Center and whipstitch bottom
edges of Trellis to base.

4. Make small carnations using silk ribbon: 34
white, 44 rose, 44 light blue and 30 taupe.
Make leaves from green ribbon.

Remove pearls from strand one at a time and
attach to each cross-section of trellis (see ● on

graph). Embellish Base and front Archway
with carnations, leaves, remaining light blue
and taupe ribbons, and remaining strand of
pearl beads (see photo).

Codes

Stitch on clear Plastic Canvas 7 over one bar.

	Cut Size
Archway (cut and stitch two)	9" x 9"
Trellis (cut and stitch two)	12" x 12"
Base Band (cut and stitch one)	25" x 5"

Stitch on clear Plastic Canvas 9" circles (see Suppliers).

| Base Top (cut and stitch one) | 7⅛" wide |
| Base Bottom (cut and stitch one) | 7⅛" wide |

STEP 1: Backstitch (three strands)

Skeins		Paternayan Persian Yarn
14		246 Neutral Gray

STEP 2: Parisian stitch (three strands). To make
Base Band, stitch 156 x 19 stitches. There is no
graph for this piece.

 246   Neutral Gray

STEP 3: Long stitch (three strands). Stitch Base
Bottom as follows:

Row One—Beginning one bar from outside edge,
stitch over six bars toward center. Repeat around
entire circle.

Row Two—Stitch toward center over next six
bars. Repeat around entire circle.

Row Three—Stitch toward center over next five
bars. Repeat around entire circle.

Row Four—Stitch toward center over next three
bars. Repeat around entire circle.

Row Five—Stitch over remaining two bars.

 246   Neutral Gray

STEP 4: Trim and overcast (three strands)

Skeins

Paternayan Persian Yarn

1

515   Old Blue-vy. lt. (Base Top and Base Bottom, See Step 2 of Directions)

246   Neutral Gray (inner edge of Archways, inner edge of small archway on Trellises)

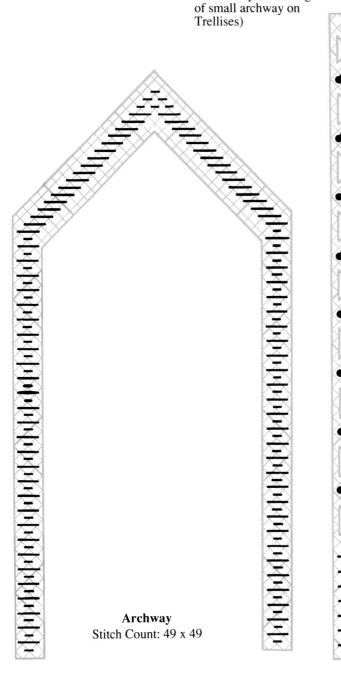

Archway
Stitch Count: 49 x 49

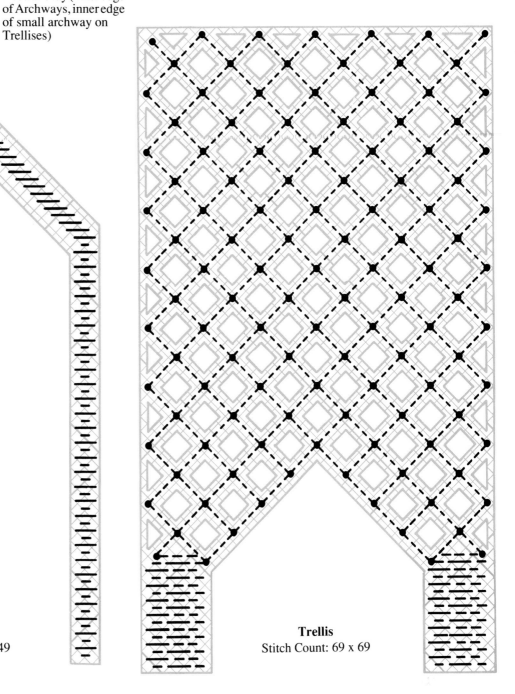

Trellis
Stitch Count: 69 x 69

Y is for the young-at-heart dream house you can build,
It's new, and it's painted in cream and peach and beige and old sky blue.
It is lovely, it is cozy, and it's what is sure to be
When dreams come true, and you do say you'll share your life with me.

▦ Your Blue Haven ▦

Finished size: 8½" W x 14½" H x 7½" D

Materials

Materials for stitching (see Codes)
1 Bottom from unstitched clear
    Plastic Canvas 7 (see graph,
    pg. 140)
1½ yards of 3"-wide flat cream lace
¼ yard of light blue crepe satin
1 (2' x 2') piece of ⅛"-wide Masonite
Wood glue
Glue gun and glue
Saw

Directions

1. Stitch and trim plastic canvas pieces as directed in Codes.

2. To make house shell, overcast the right long edge to the left long edge of the following Shell pieces in alphabetical order: A, B, all three Cs, D, E, and F. Overcast edges of A and F together. Overcast all top edges of shell.

3. To make porch, overcast top edge of C to bottom of A. Overcast remaining porch pieces together (Diagram 1).

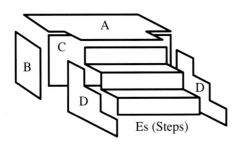

Diagram 1

Overcast assembled porch to Front A and Front B (see graphs). Overcast unstitched Bottom underneath shell/porch.

4. To add embellishments, cut one 3" x 4" piece from lace and satin. Layer lace and satin, then glue behind front door inside shell, with lace showing through windows.

   Cut 16 3" x 3" pieces from satin and lace. Gather and glue one layer of lace/satin behind each window with lace showing through.

   Center and glue one Window Cap above each window (see photo). Glue grayish edge of Lower Awning above lower bay windows at each ● (see graph).

5. To make balcony, overcast balcony pieces together (Diagram 2). Glue to Front A and Front B of shell at each ● (see graphs).

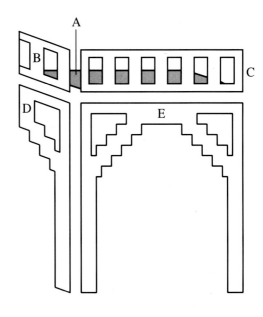

Diagram 2

6. To make insert, cut the following pieces from Masonite: two 10½" x 8" (Front and Back), two 10½" x 3⅝" (Sides), and one 8½" x 3½" (Bottom). Glue pieces together to form a rectangle with an open top. Place inside house shell.

7. To make dormer, overcast Dormer pieces as follows: Bs to each side of A, Ds to each side of C. Overcast top edges of D/C/D. Overcast E to lower edge of D/C/D (Diagram 3).

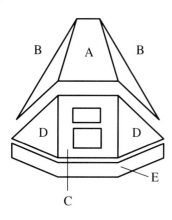

Diagram 3

Cut one 2" x 3" piece of lace and satin; gather and glue inside windows, with lace facing out. Glue top edge of D/C/D/E underneath B/A/B.

8. To make roof, overcast top edges of both Roofs together. Whipstitch dormer to roof (see graph for placement). Place wrong side of Soffit underneath roof, aligning all edges. Overcast all edges of Soffit, catching roof/dormer in stitches. Insert one Gable ½" inside each open end of roof; glue. Glue roof to top of house shell. Glue one Corbel underneath Soffit at each corner.

Codes

Stitch on Plastic Canvas 7.

	Cut Sizes:
Shell:	
A (cut and stitch one)	6" x 12"
B (cut and stitch one)	3" x 12"
C (cut and stitch three)	4" x 12"
D (cut and stitch one)	7" x 12"
E (cut and stitch one)	10" x 12"
F (cut and stitch one)	6" x 12"
Porch:	
A (cut and stitch one)	6" x 3"
B (cut and stitch one)	3" x 3"
C (cut and stitch one)	6" x 3"
D (cut and stitch two)	3" x 3"
E (cut and stitch five)	5" x 3"
Embellishments:	
Window Cap	3" x 3"
(cut and stitch 15)	
Lower Awning	8" x 3"
(cut and stitch one)	
Corbels	3" x 3"
(cut and stitch eight)	
Balcony:	
A (cut and stitch one)	6" x 3"
B (cut and stitch one)	3" x 3"
C (cut and stitch one)	6" x 3"
D (cut and stitch one)	3" x 6"
E (cut and stitch one)	6" x 6"
Dormer:	
A (cut and stitch one)	4" x 6"
B (cut and stitch two)	5" x 6"
C (cut and stitch one)	4" x 4"
D (cut and stitch one of each)	4" x 4"
E (cut and stitch one)	9" x 3"
Roof:	
Roof (cut and stitch two)	12" x 7"
Soffit (cut and stitch one)	10" x 10"
Gable (cut and stitch two)	7" x 5"

STEP 1: Continental and reverse continental stitch (one strand)

Skeins

Windrush Yarn

9077   Pale Taupe

90111   Lt. Powder Blue

DMC Floss

3773   Pecan-vy. lt. (12 strands)

Cards

8

Overture

V38   Metals

STEP 2: Long stitch (one strand)

Windrush Yarn

9077   Pale Taupe

90111   Lt. Powder Blue

DMC Floss

3773   Pecan-vy. lt. (12 strands)

3773   Pecan-vy. lt. (six strands)

STEP 3: Backstitch (six strands)

3773   Pecan-vy. lt.

STEP 4: Short stitch (one strand)

Windrush Yarn

9077   Pale Taupe

STEP 5: Smyrna cross stitch (12 strands)

Skeins

DMC Floss

3712   Salmon-med.

STEP 6: Modified fir stitch (one strand)

Overture

V38   Metals

STEP 7: Straight stitch (one strand)

V38   Metals

STEP 8: Compensation stitch (one strand)

V38   Metals

STEP 9: Trim and overcast (one strand)

Windrush Yarn

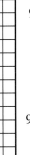

9077   Pale Taupe (all windows except dormer and door windows; shell (see Step 2 of Directions; outer edge of Lower Awning)

90111   Lt. Powder Blue (door windows; Gables; shell, see Step 2 of Directions; Bottom, see Step 3 of Directions; dormer, see Step 7 of Directions)

DMC Floss

3773   Pecan-vy. lt. (12 strands) (Corbels, Window Caps; porch, see Step 3 of Directions)

Overture

V38   Metals (inner edge of Lower Awning; roof and Soffit, see Step 8 of Directions)

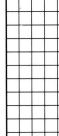

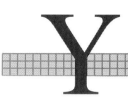

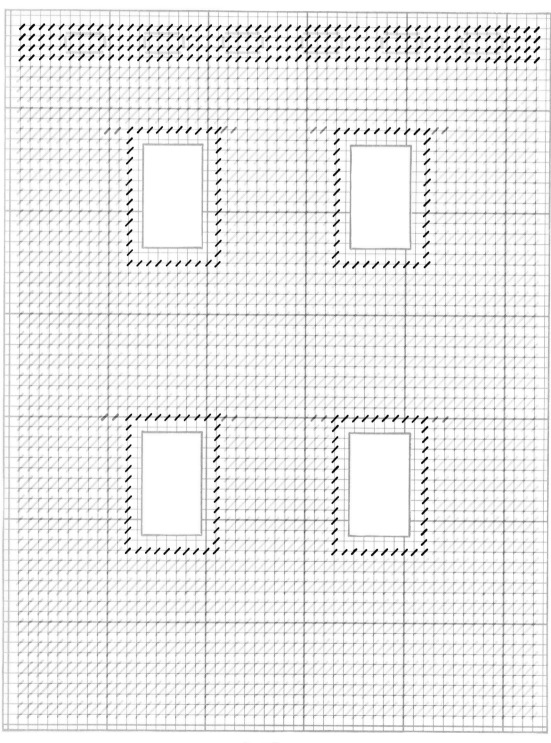

Shell E
Stitch Count: 55 x 70

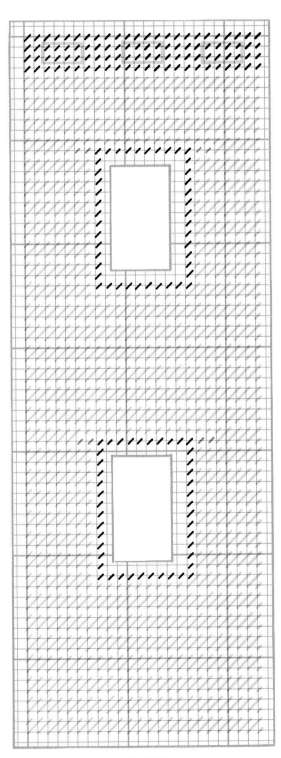

Shell F
Stitch Count: 26 x 70

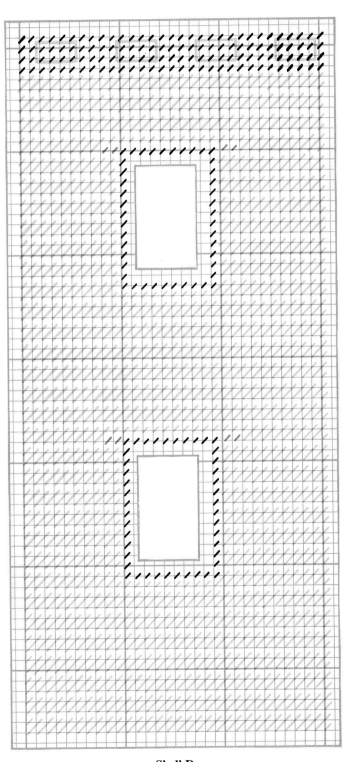

Shell D
Stitch Count: 33 x 70

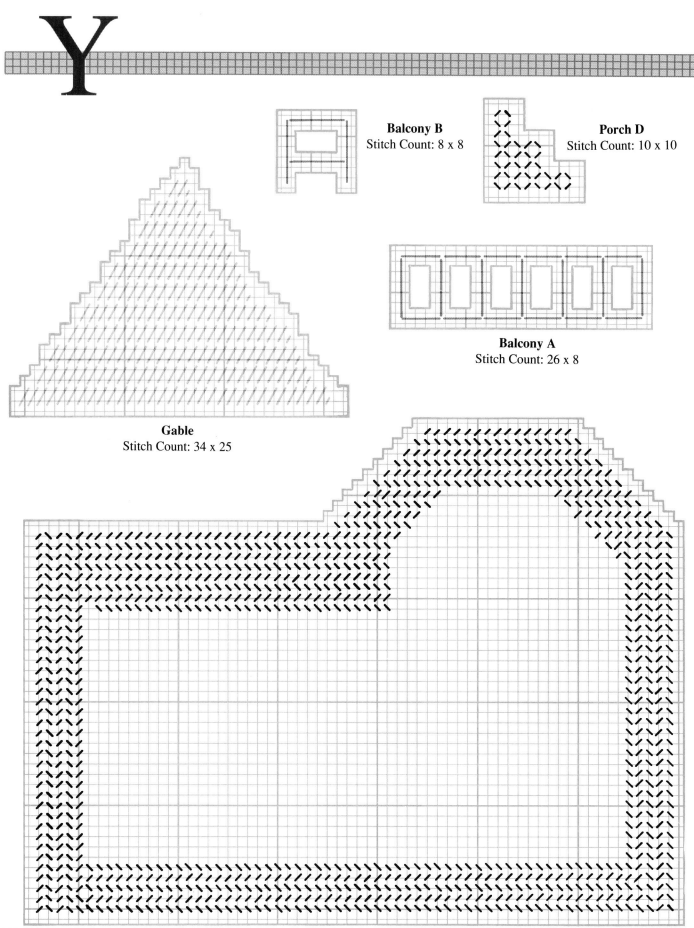

Balcony B
Stitch Count: 8 x 8

Porch D
Stitch Count: 10 x 10

Balcony A
Stitch Count: 26 x 8

Gable
Stitch Count: 34 x 25

Soffit
Stitch Count: 49 x 66

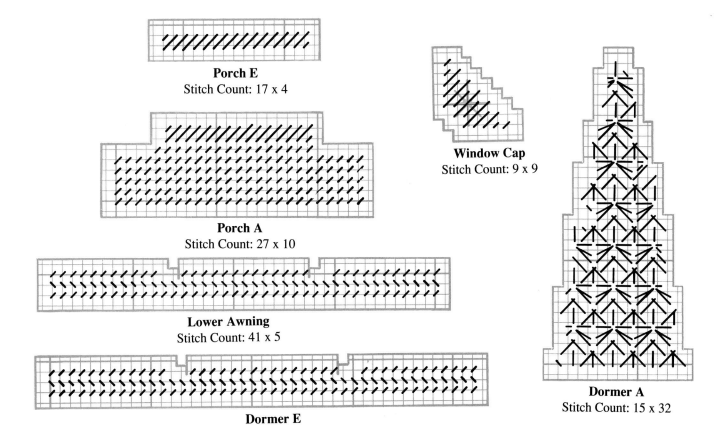

Porch E
Stitch Count: 17 x 4

Porch A
Stitch Count: 27 x 10

Window Cap
Stitch Count: 9 x 9

Lower Awning
Stitch Count: 41 x 5

Dormer E
Stitch Count: 45 x 5

Dormer A
Stitch Count: 15 x 32

Roof
Stitch Count: 66 x 32

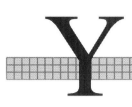

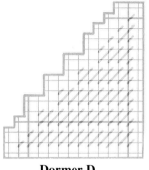

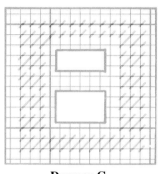

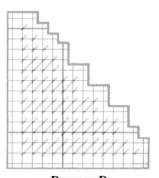

Dormer D
Stitch Count: 14 x 15

Dormer C
Stitch Count: 15 x 15

Dormer D
Stitch Count: 14 x 15

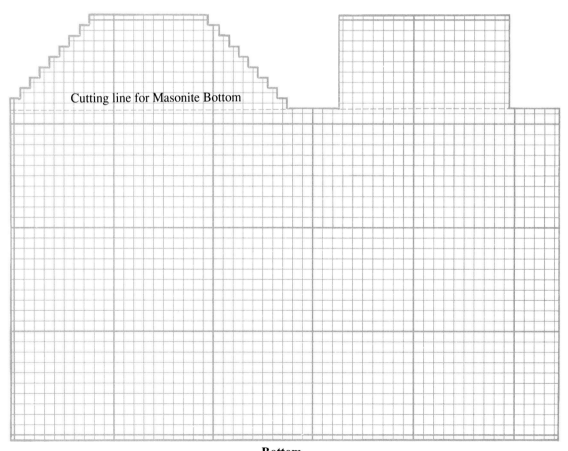

Cutting line for Masonite Bottom

Bottom
Stitch Count: 55 x 42

Corbel
Stitch Count: 5 x 10

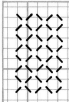

Porch B
Stitch Count: 7 x 10

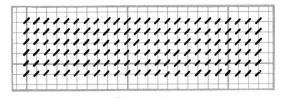

Porch C
Stitch Count: 27 x 10

Balcony C
Stitch Count: 26 x 8

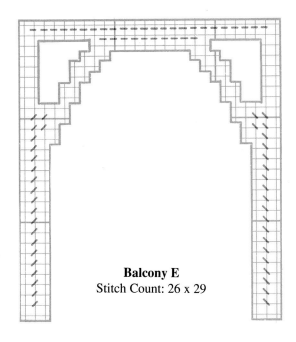

Balcony E
Stitch Count: 26 x 29

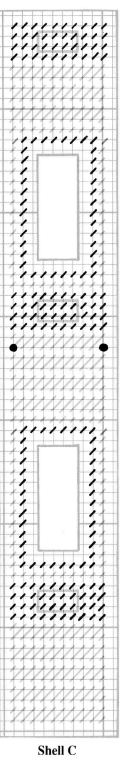

Shell C
Stitch Count: 12 x 70

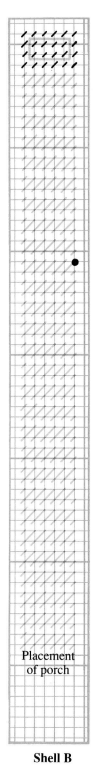

Placement
of porch

Shell B
Stitch Count: 8 x 70

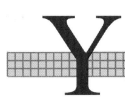

Dormer B
Stitch Count: 21 x 29

Dormer B
Stitch Count: 21 x 29

Balcony D
Stitch Count: 7 x 29

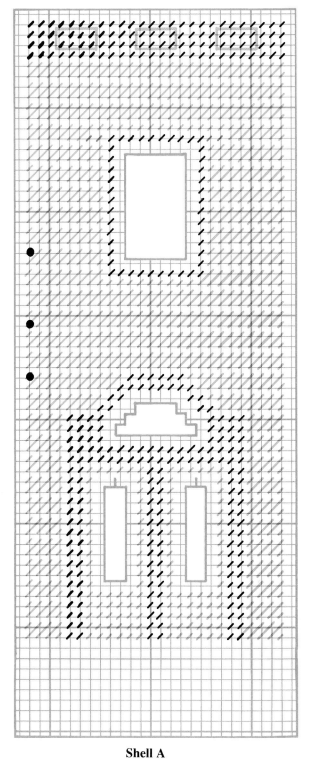

Shell A
Stitch Count: 28 x 70

 **Z** Z is for zenana—a box that is so fine,
I'd rather have it made than a bottle of fine red wine.
It must be for a lady who is noble and so true,
And is a harem lady; please do say, would that be you?

A Zenana Box

Finished size: 6½" W x 3½" H

Materials

Materials for stitching (see Codes)
2 (9" x 9") pieces of clear Plastic Canvas 10
½ yard of green satin
1 letter-sized Manila folder
1 (14" x 8") piece of fleece
Tacky Glue (see Suppliers)
Tape

Directions

1. Stitch and trim plastic canvas pieces as directed in Codes.

2. To make lid, use stitched Top as a pattern and cut one from each of the following: unstitched plastic canvas (unstitched Top); satin, adding ½" seam allowances on all edges (satin Top); and fleece, omitting ¼" on all edges (fleece Top).

   From satin, cut one 23" x 2⅜" piece (satin Rim). From Manila folder, cut two 11" x 1⅜" pieces. Mark score lines at 2¾" intervals. Tape two short ends together with edges flush to make a 22" piece (Manila Rim). Crease along score lines. Set aside.

   Overcast short edges of Rim Panels together. Place unstitched Top on wrong side of stitched Top. Overcast pieced rim to Tops, with stitching facing out. Overcast all remaining edges.

3. Glue fleece Top to wrong side of pieced lid. Center wrong side of satin Top against fleece; glue, pulling each side of satin smoothly over fleece.

   Center Manila Rim on wrong side of satin Rim. Fold satin over all edges of Manila, gluing on back. Allow to dry. Crease again along score lines. Glue to wrong side of lid's rim, matching seams and creases.

4. To make box, use stitched Bottom as a pattern to cut one unstitched plastic canvas Bottom, one satin Bottom and one fleece Bottom (see Step 2).

   From satin, cut one 22" x 4" piece (satin Box). From Manila folder, cut two 10½" x 3" pieces. Mark scores lines at 2⅝" intervals. Tape two short ends together with edges flush to make a 21" piece (Manila Box). Crease along score lines. Set aside.

   Overcast long edges of Box Sides together. Place unstitched Bottom on wrong side of stitched Bottom. Overcast pieced sides to Bottoms, with stitching facing out. Overcast all remaining edges.

5. Line box using fleece Bottom, satin Bottom, satin Box and Manila Box (see Step 3).

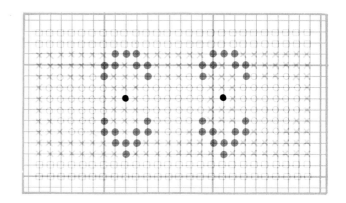

Rim Panel
Stitch Count: 28 x 16

Codes

Stitch on clear Plastic Canvas 10 over one bar.

	Cut Size
Top (cut and stitch one)	9" x 9"
Rim Panel (cut and stitch eight)	5" x 4"
Box Side (cut and stitch eight)	5" x 6"
Bottom (cut and stitch one, see STEP 2 below)	9" x 9"

STEP 1: Cross-stitch (four strands)

Skeins		Marlitt	
1	—	1012	Off White
1	▫	1013	Yellow-lt. pale
1	–	1019	Salmon-lt.
1	⊙	830	Rose-lt.
1	–	879	Rose-med.
2	⊙	831	Salmon-med.
1	▫	881	Rose
1	✕	893	Christmas Red
1	●	894	Garnet
1	✕	1007	Lavender-lt.
1	●	858	Violet-dk.
3	▫	832	Nile Green-med.
21	◈	834	Emerald Green-vy. dk.

		DMC Floss	
3	✕	369	Pistachio Green-vy. lt.

STEP 2: Cross-stitch Bottom (four strands) Cross-stitch 64 x 64 stitches the same shape as the Top, omitting the outside row of stitches. There is no graph. Trim one bar outside stitching.

Marlitt

834	Emerald Green-vy. dk.

STEP 3: Trim and overcast (four strands)

834	Emerald Green-vy. dk. (See Steps 2 and 4 of Directions)

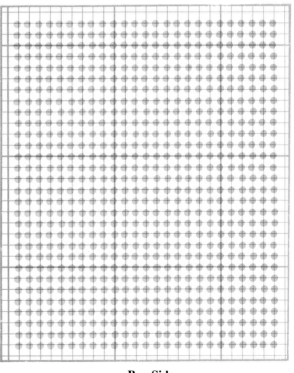

Box Side
Stitch Count: 27 x 32

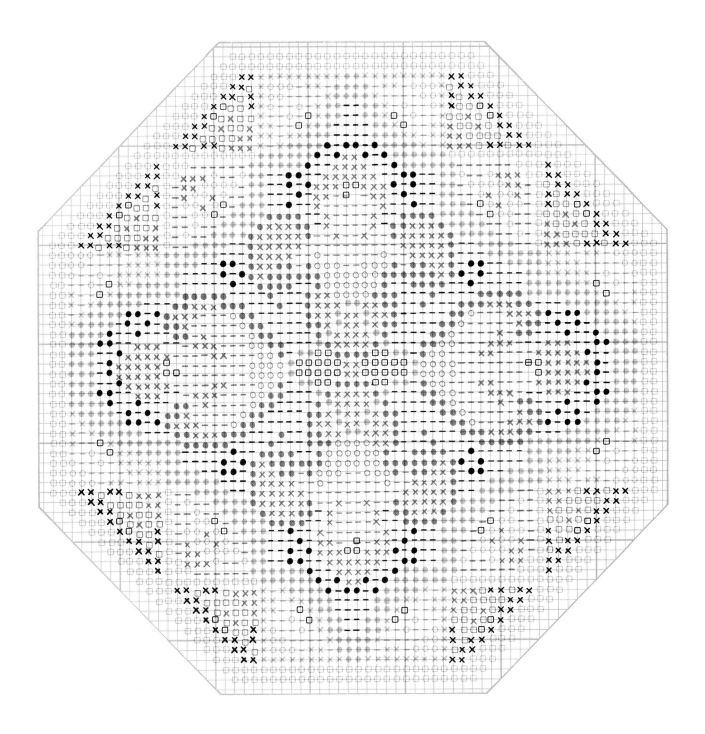

Top
Stitch Count: 66 x 66

General Instructions

Plastic canvas is a molded, nonwoven canvas made from clear or colored plastic, consisting of "bars" with "holes" in between. It comes in mesh sizes 7, 10 and 14, which refer to the number of holes in 1" of canvas. Each size is used in this book. In addition, plastic canvas comes in various sizes, shapes and colors: 4" x 4" squares, 12" x 18" rectangles, by the yard from a roll, circles, diamonds, cream, white, or green, just to name a few.

Some of our projects use round plastic canvas with holes radiating from the center. As it has no mesh size, it is identified by its diameter. For example, some projects will call for a 3", 6" or 9" circle. It is important to purchase the specific size called for.

To order 7 or 10 mesh and round plastic canvas directly, write to Darice Incorporated; to order cream 14 mesh (available in 4" x 4" squares only) write to Chapelle Designers (see Suppliers).

SUPPLIES NEEDED

Plastic canvas: See the project Codes and Materials list for the size, color and amount needed.

Tapestry needles: They need to be small enough for the mesh size and yet have eyes large enough to accommodate the number of strands used. A #24 tapestry needle is the standard size used in the majority of plastic canvas projects.

Stitching materials: See the project Directions and Codes for specifics. Often DMC floss, yarn, ribbon, braid, cord and other specialty threads are called for. Always check the list of Suppliers

for information on where to purchase these threads if they are not available locally. Although the suppliers we've listed only sell wholesale, your local merchant will be able to order them for you. Colors, number of strands used and the amounts needed are always listed in the Codes.

Cutting materials: You will need sharp scissors and/or an X-acto knife, unless otherwise specified in the project materials list.

Glues: Tacky glue (see Suppliers), hot glue and glue sticks, and wood glue are often needed to construct a project. They will be called for in the project materials list.

Tracing paper and pencil: See "Making a pattern" below.

PROJECT INSTRUCTIONS

Instructions to complete each project are divided into three sections, outlined below:

Directions: The Directions section lists all the materials needed, as well as finishing instructions, to complete the project. If there is no Directions section included, completion of the project is covered in the Codes (see below).

Graph: The graph is a symbol picture of the piece to be stitched. Each line is the equivalent of one bar of plastic canvas. Each symbol shows you where to actually make the stitches, and is cross-referenced in the Codes bar.

Codes: The first paragraph of the Codes includes the type of plastic canvas used, including color and mesh; the size to cut the canvas before stitching; and the number of pieces to stitch.

Next are the instructions to actually stitch the project. They are listed in steps, which should be completed sequentially. Also listed are the stitching materials, brand names, quantities, and color by names and numbers, as well as the stitches used. It should be noted that the first time each new stitching material used is listed, the amount called for is enough to complete the entire project.

Unless otherwise specified, the last step in the Codes is the trim and overcast step. This step does not have a symbol, but is indicated by the thick black lines on the graph. It is a guide to show where to cut out and overcast your stitched piece. Be sure to read the Codes before overcasting; often you will be referred to the Directions for special instructions.

CUTTING

Once a piece has been stitched, carefully cut in the space between the two unstitched bars indicated by the trim and overcast line on the graph. Trim the remaining nubs.

Also, cut all corners on the diagonal, but not so close that they weaken (Diagram 1); this makes finishing the edges easier.

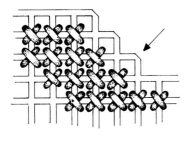

Diagram 1

STITCHING TIPS

To begin stitching, do not make a knot at the end of thread. Instead, bring the needle up from the back, leaving a 1" piece of thread. Hold the piece in place while making a few stitches over it. If there is an adjacent area already stitched, weave the thread through the back to secure either beginning or ending stitches.

Always practice any unfamiliar stitches before beginning (see Special Stitches, pages 150 - 158). Also, when possible, work light areas first. This prevents the fuzz from darker areas being pulled into them.

Always allow two empty grids outside stitching. Except when a piece of plastic canvas has been called for by the number of bars, all cut sizes (see *Codes* above) allow for a 2" margin around the stitching; therefore, when the number of bars has been given, there is no need to allow for the 2" margin.

Keep stitching tension consistent to insure that each stitch lies flat and even on the canvas. If the tension is too tight, the canvas will show between the stitches. If it is too loose, the thread will not lie flat, causing the bars of the canvas to show through.

SEWING TECHNIQUES

Making a pattern: Outline the stitched plastic canvas piece on tracing paper with a pencil.

Enlarging a pattern: Choose paper large enough for the finished pattern size. Mark grid lines 1" apart on the paper or use graph paper with a 1" grid. Begin marking dots on 1" grid lines where the reduced pattern intersects the corresponding grid line. Connect the dots. Also available is pattern-enlarging fabric (Pattern Pellon™), which has small dots at 1" intervals.

Marking on fabric: Use a washable dressmakers' pen or chalk to mark on fabric.

Clipping and trimming: Clipping seam allowances is necessary on all curves, points and most corners so that the finished seam will lie flat. Clip into the seam allowance at even intervals, ¼" to ½" apart, being careful not to cut through the stitching. Trim seam allowance to ⅛" when too bulky.

RIBBON FLOWERS AND LEAVES

Large rose: Cut an 18" piece of ribbon. Fold ribbon at the center to form a right angle (Diagram 2). Continue folding the ribbon back and forth, keeping the right angle, alternating the ends, and placing each layer on top of the previous layers (Diagram 3 and 4). Make 15 to 20 folds.

  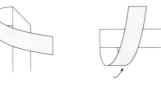

Diagram 2　　　Diagram 3　　　Diagram 4

Holding ends securely, release the top (Diagram 5). Pull gently on the longer end to gather up the rose. Push threaded needle through center of the rose, securing all layers. Cut end of ribbon, leaving a ¼" tail for attaching.

Diagram 5

Large carnation: Cut a 4" piece of ribbon. Tie a knot at one end of the ribbon. With tweezers, pull one thread from the center of the opposite end until the ribbon gathers to the knot. Untie the knot and trim the end to ⅛". Glue the ends of the ribbon to the back of the flower.

Leaf: Cut a 2" piece of ribbon. Place the ribbon wrong side up on a flat surface. Fold right, then left sides forward to form a point (Diagram 6). Hand stitch a gathering thread as shown. Gather tightly and secure, trimming any excess ribbon (Diagram 7).

Diagram 6

Diagram 7

CARING FOR FINISHED PROJECTS

Pieces stitched with acrylic yarn, embroidery thread or other specialty threads can be hand washed in warm water with a mild detergent or in cold water with a cold-water detergent. Do not rub or scrub the stitches; rubbing causes threads to fuzz. Rinse pieces thoroughly and allow to dry. Do not put them in a clothes dryer as the heat can cause the plastic to melt. Also, plastic canvas cannot be dry cleaned because chemicals used in the process dissolve it. When a piece has dried, trim off any fuzz with a small pair of sharp scissors.

Special Stitches

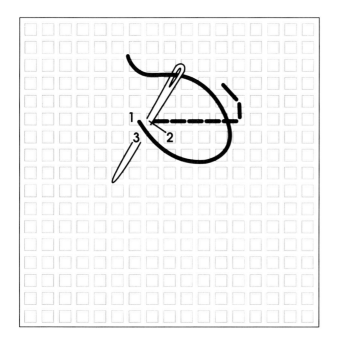

BACKSTITCH

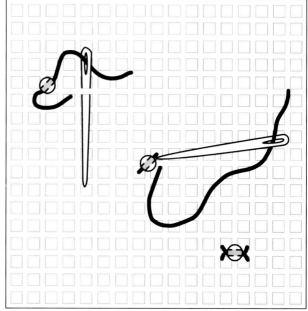

BEADWORK

BACKSTITCH: Work stitches from left to right. Bring needle up at 1, down at 2, and up again at 3.

BEADWORK: Bring the needle up at lower left corner at point where bead is to be placed. Thread one bead on the needle and push needle down in upper right corner of placement point. (For beads to lie properly, all stitches must go in same direction.) Straighten bead by going back through center.

BOSNIA STITCH: Begin by stitching a row of vertical stitches, working from right to left. Connect these with diagonal stitches, forming backward Ns. Always point the needle downward as it moves under canvas.

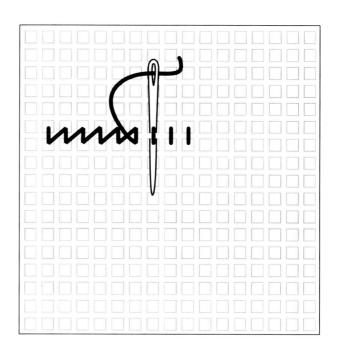

BOSNIA STITCH

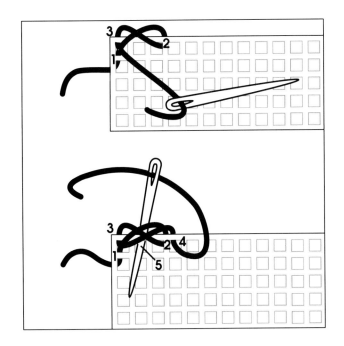

BRAIDED CROSS-STITCH

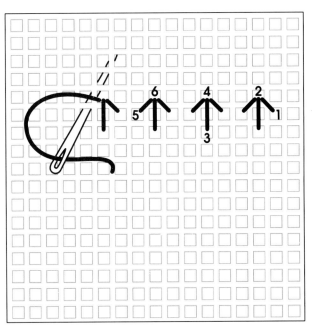

COMPENSATION STITCH

CONTINENTAL STITCH

BRAIDED CROSS-STITCH VARIATION:
Beginning at one corner, bring needle up at 1.
Take thread over edge of canvas and bring
needle up at 2. Take thread over previous stitch
and bring needle up at 3. Take thread over
stitching and bring needle up at 4.

COMPENSATION STITCH: This is any
stitch where space allows for only part of the
whole stitch. The diagram above is helpful with
the fir stitch. Bring needle up at 1, down at 2,
up at 3, down at 4. Then bring needle up at 5
and down at 6.

CONTINENTAL STITCH: Follow sequence
indicated by numbers in diagram, bringing the
needle up at odd numbers and down at even
numbers.

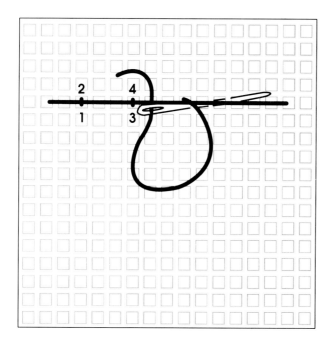

COUCHING

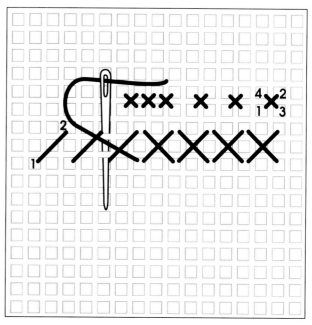

CROSS-STITCH

COUCHING: Bring needle up at 1 then down at 2 to couch over the laid thread. The couching thread and the laid thread may be the same or different threads.

CROSS-STITCH: Bring needle up at 1, down at 2, up at 3, and down again at 4. To stitch rows, work from left to right and then back.

DOUBLE CROSS-STITCH: Follow the sequence indicated by numbers in diagram, bringing needle up at odd numbers and down at even numbers.

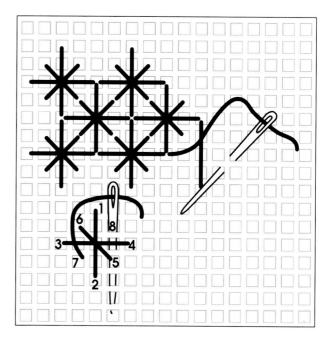

DOUBLE CROSS-STITCH

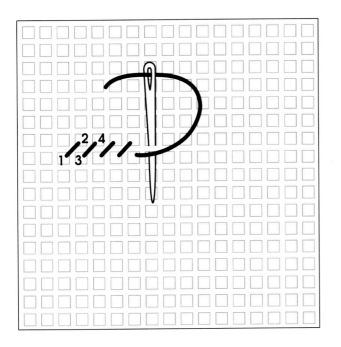

HALF CROSS-STITCH

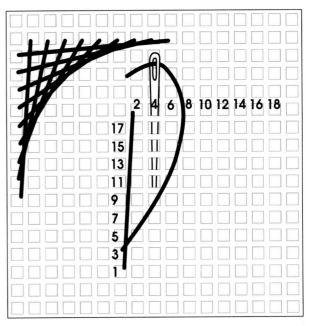

JESSICA STITCH

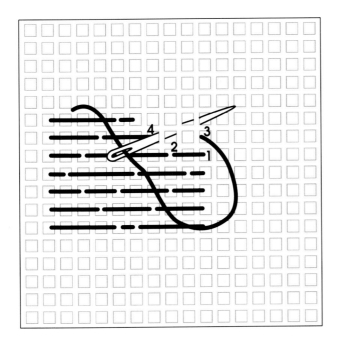

LONG STITCH

HALF CROSS-STITCH: Bring needle up at 1 and down at 2. Repeat as needed.

JESSICA STITCH: Follow sequence indicated by numbers in diagram, bringing needle up at odd numbers and down at even numbers.

LONG STITCH: Bring needle up at 1, down at 2. Then bring needle up at 3 and down at 4. Continue sequence, staggering stitches in adjacent rows.

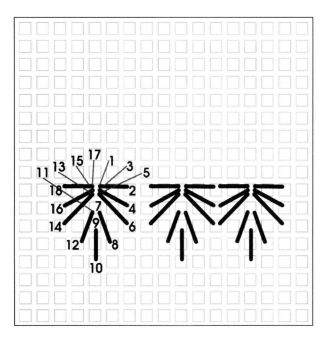

MODIFIED FIR STITCH

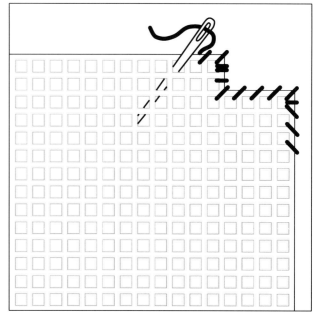

OVERCAST STITCH

MODIFIED FIR STITCH: Follow sequence indicated by numbers in diagram, bringing needle up at odd numbers and down at even numbers.

OVERCAST STITCH: Working in either direction, make evenly spaced and slanted diagonal stitches to cover canvas edges and corners or as needed to join two sections together.

PADDED LONG STITCH: Make stitches in layers following sequence indicated by numbers in diagram, bringing needle up at odd numbers and down at even numbers. The bold black lines indicate the first layer.

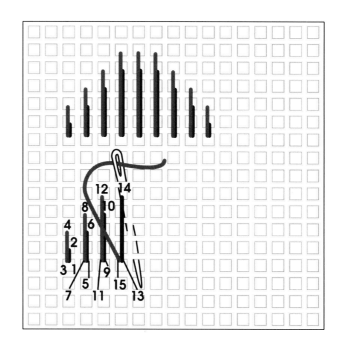

PADDED LONG STITCH

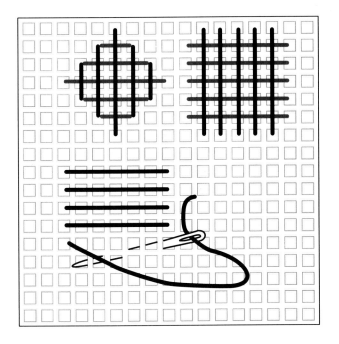

PADDED SATIN STITCH

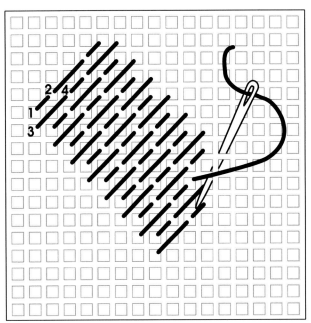

PARISIAN STITCH

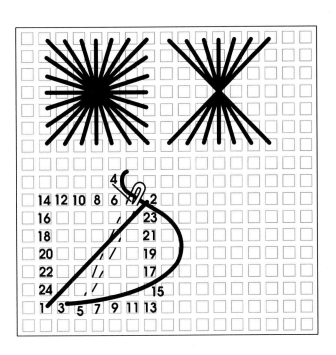

RHODES STITCH

PADDED SATIN STITCH: Make satin stitches in layers, with first layer in one direction and next layer stitched over first in opposite direction. For second layer, pass needle between canvas and first layer of stitching. The gray lines indicate the first layer.

PARISIAN STITCH: Work stitches in an alternating pattern and over one or two bars. Begin by making a small stitch, bringing needle up at 1 and down at 2. Then make a longer stitch, bringing needle up at 3 and down at 4.

RHODES STITCH: Make stitches following sequence indicated by numbers in diagram, bringing needle up at odd numbers and down at even numbers.

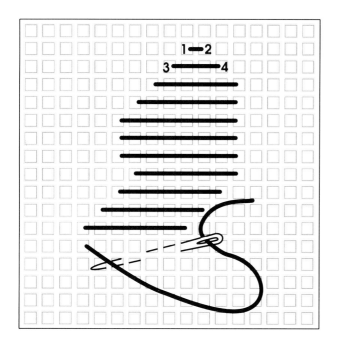

SATIN STITCH

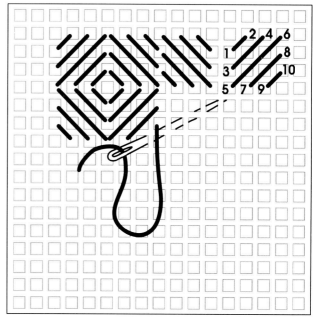

SCOTCH STITCH

SATIN STITCH: Bring needle up at left edge of design (1) and down at right edge of design (2). Then bring needle up again at 3 and down at 4, one bar below first stitch. Make stitches lay close together and flat.

SCOTCH STITCH: Make diagonal stitches to form a square. Work first stitch over one bar, bringing needle up at 1 and down at 2. Fill in square with diagonal stitches varying in size. Alternating the direction of the squares creates a secondary pattern.

SHORT STITCH: To make stitches in a row, bring needle up at 1 and down at 2. Stitches can also be worked in diagonal designs. Make stitches following sequence, bringing needle up at odd numbers and down at even numbers.

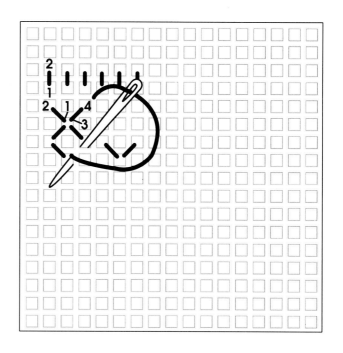

SHORT STITCH

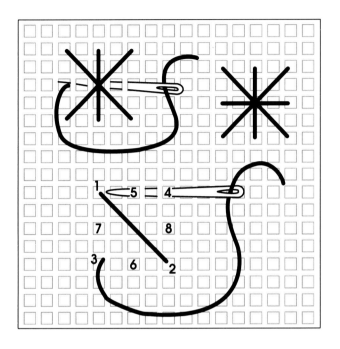

SMYRNA CROSS-STITCH

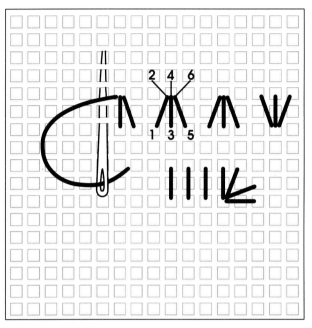

STRAIGHT STITCH

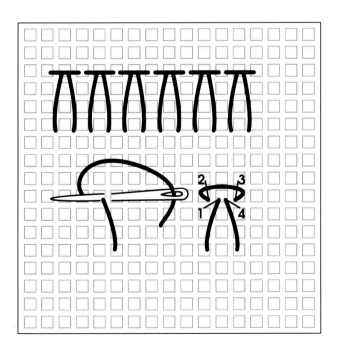

TURKISH TUFTING

SMYRNA CROSS-STITCH: Begin by making a cross-stitch , bringing needle up at 1, down at 2, up at 3 and down at 4. Then make a straight cross over cross-stitch, bringing needle up at 5, down at 6, up at 7 and down at 8.

STRAIGHT STITCH: Make stitches following sequence indicated by numbers, bringing needle up at odd numbers and down at even numbers.

TURKISH TUFTING: Take needle down at 1, up at 2, down at 3 and up at 4. Pull the thread firmly downward until a tight knot is made. Then pull all threads up. Trim threads as needed to create an even pile.

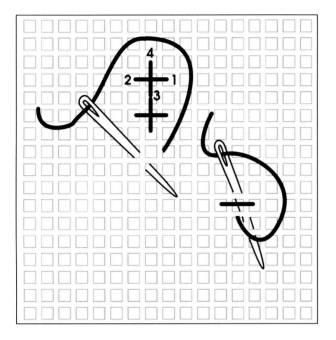

UPRIGHT CROSS-STITCH

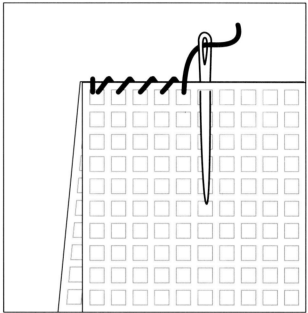

WHIPSTITCH

UPRIGHT CROSS-STITCH: Bring needle up at 1, down at 2, up at 3 and down at 4.

WHIPSTITCH: Make small slanted stitches over the overcast edges of two sections to join them together.

WOVEN STITCH: Make stitches in over-under woven layers following sequence indicated by numbers, bringing needle up at odd numbers and down at even numbers. Bold black lines indicate layer to be stitched first. Gray lines indicate second layer to be woven through first.

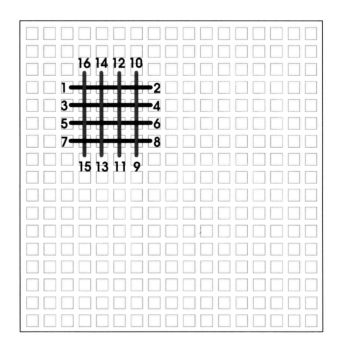

WOVEN STITCH

Suppliers

All products except plastic canvas are available retail from Shepherd's Bush, 220 24th Street, Ogden, UT 84401. Or, for a merchant near you, write to the following suppliers:

Cotonella Yarn
Aarlan
27452 Crestview Ct.
Farmington Hills, MI 48331

Procelain-ize-it, Tacky Glue
Aleene's Division of Artis, Inc.
85 Industrial Way
Buellton, CA 93427

Curly Roving
All Cooped Up Designs
560 S. State #B-1
Orem, UT 84058

Windrush Yarn
Brunswick Worsted Mills, Inc.
P. O. Box 276
Pickens, SC 29671

Watercolours Thread
The Caron Collection
67 Poland St.
Bridgeport, CT 06605

Jack-in-the-box Ceramic Head, cream Plastic Canvas 14, Music Box Movement #570, Music Box Movement with Waggie #571, Music Box Movement with Base #572
Chapelle Designers
Box 9252, Newgate Station
Ogden, UT 84409

Acadia Yarn
Classic Elite Yarns
12 Perkins Street
Lowell, MA 01854

Plastic Canvas Circles: 3" —#33005, 6" —#337816, 9"— #33027
Darice Incorporated
21160 Drake Road
Strongville, OH 44136

Matte Cotton, Pearl Cotton, Floss
The DMC Corporation
Port Kearny Building #10
South Kearny, NJ 07032-0650 U.S.A.

Setacolor Paint/Dye
Dharma Trading Company
Box 916
San Rafael, CA 94915

Narrow French Grosgrain Ribbon
Elsie's Exquisiques
513 Broadway
Niles, MI 49120

Glass and Pebble Beads: Mill Hill Beads
Mill Hill Division of Gay Bowles Sales, Inc.
P. O. Box 1060
Janesville, WI 53547

Paternayan Yarn
Johnson Creative Arts, Inc.
P.O. Box 158
445 Main St.
West Townsend, MA 01474-0158

French Ribbon
Princess Ribbon Corp.
3320 Tait Ter
Norfolk, VA 23513

Balger Products/Threads
Kreinik Manufacturing Co., Inc.
P.O. Box 1966
1708 Gihon Road
Parkersburg, WV 26102

Glissen Gloss Threads, including Estaz
Madeira Marketing Ltd.
600 E. 9th, Third Floor
Michigan City, IN 46360

Gold Lamé Thread
Mangelsen's
P.O. Box 3314
Department PCD060
Omaha, NE 68103

Spring Thread
Needle Necessities
P.O. Box 8199
10922 N. E. 133rd Street
Kirkland, WA 98034

Overture, Pebbly Perle, Ultra Suede, Neon Rays, Double Gold, Patina Threads, Cresta d'Oro Thread
Rainbow Gallery
13756 Victory Boulevard
Van Nuys, CA 91401

Sew Your Wild Threads
T.S. Designs
249C Avenida del Norte
Redondo Beach, CA 90277

Silk Ribbon
YLI Corporation
P.O. Box 109 (mail orders)
482 Freedom Boulevard (inquiries)
Provo, UT 84603 and 84601 respectively

Marlitt
Zweigart Fabrics/Joan Toggitt Ltd.
Weston Canal Plaza
2 Riverview Drive
Somerset, NJ 08873

Index

All of us at Meredith® Press are dedicated to offering you, our customer, the best books we can create. We are particularly concerned that all of the instructions for making projects are clear and accurate. Please address your correspondence to: Customer Service Department, Meredith® Press, Meredith Corporation, 150 East 52nd Street, New York, NY 10022

If you are interested in any other titles from The Vanessa-Ann Collection or Meredith Books, please write to Meredith Books, P. O. Box 10670, Des Moines, IA 50336, or call 1-800-678-2665.